THE NEW SAT CRITICAL READING WORKBOOK

SPARK NOTES

A Division of Barnes & Noble Publishing

Spark Educational Publishing
A Division of Barnes & Noble Publishing
120 Fifth Avenue
New York, NY 10011

ISBN 1-4114-0434-3

Please submit changes or report errors to www.sparknotes.com/errors.

Printed and bound in Canada.

SAT is the registered trademark of the College Entrance Examination Board, which was not involved in the production of, and does not endorse this product.

CONTENTS

Reading Passages 51

SAT Vocabulary 131

CONTENTS

the
new SAT
Critical
Reading
Workbook

INTRODUCTION

SAT "VERBAL" IS DEAD. KAPUT. Gone the way of the Dodo and the Sega Dreamcast. Or so the SAT wants you to believe. Actually, it's more accurate to say that most of the former SAT Verbal section is just wearing a fake mustache and traveling under an assumed name: "Critical Reading." The new Critical Reading section has all the familiar sentence completion and long reading questions as the section formerly known as "SAT Verbal," but now analogies have been cut, and new *short* reading questions have been added.

VERBAL VS. CRITICAL READING

In this corner, the Verbal section! In that corner, the Critical Reading section! Here's a table that compares the new Critical Reading section and the old Verbal section.

	Old Verbal	New Critical Reading
Analogies	YES	NO
Sentence Completion	YES	YES
Long Reading Passages	YES	YES
Dual Reading Passages	YES	YES
Short Reading Passages	NO	YES

Memorizing a list of tough vocabulary words and outwitting analogies went a long way toward getting you a good score on the old SAT Verbal section. That kind of preparation just won't cut it on the new Critical Reading section. Vocabulary still plays an important role on the test, but its role has changed. Questions no longer exclusively focus on vocabulary. Questions that do include tough vocab do so within the context of a sentence or a paragraph that provides clues to what the word means.

The emphasis on vocabulary *in context* on the new SAT makes excellent critical reading skills all the more important. Learning to read critically can help you answer questions correctly even when the meaning of certain words escapes you, and that could vastly improve your score on this section. So, while you should still study vocab (and we've got a list of the toughest words and techniques on how to remember them at the end of this section), you should also build up your reading muscles. And there's only one way to build up your muscles—exercise.

THE NEED TO READ

The best way to prepare for the Critical Reading section is to read. From the moment you read this sentence until the day you take the SAT, you should carve time out of your life to read. Read magazines. Read newspapers. Read books.

You already know how to read. But for the new SAT, you have to read *critically*, and that's a different skill. You need to develop an eye and an ear for the kinds of things the Critical Reading section tests:

- **Main idea**: What is the main subject of the passage?
- **Argument**: What position does the author take on the subject? What is the main *purpose* of the passage?
- **Tone**: What is the author's attitude or feelings toward the subject?
- **Technique**: What rhetorical devices (simile, metaphor, personification, etc.) does the author use to convey his or her tone, main ideas, and argument?

In our chapter "The Long of It," we offer tips on how to turn ordinary reading into productive Critical Reading preparation. We show you how to train your *critical* reading muscles so that when the SAT comes around, all you'll have to do is flex.

BASIC FACTS

The Critical Reading section is made up of three timed sections that test your critical reading skills for 70 minutes. Two of the timed sections are 25-minutes long, and one is 20 minutes long.

In all, the Critical Reading sections contain 67 questions.

- **19 Sentence Completions**: Single sentences with one or two blanks.
- **8 Short Reading questions**: Two single passages followed by 2 questions each; one dual passage followed by 4 questions
- **40 Long Reading questions** : A 400-500 word passage with 6 questions; a 500-600 word passage with 9 questions; a 700-800 word passagewith 12 questions; a dual passage with 13 questions.

The different types of questions break into the three timed sections in the following way:

- **25-minute Section with 24 Total Questions**: 8 Sentence Completions; 2 Short Reading Comp passages (each with 2 questions); Long Reading Comp passage with 12 questions.
- **25-minute Section with 24 Total Questions**: 5 Sentence Completions; the dual Short Reading Comp passage with 4 questions; Long Reading Comp with 6 questions; Long Reading Comp with 9 questions.
- **20-minute Section with 19 Total Questions**: 6 Sentence Completions; Long Reading Dual passage with 13 questions.

On some versions of the test the 800-word Long Reading Comp and the Dual Passage Long Reading Comp switch positions. When this happens, the 800-word LRC has 13 questions, while the Dual has 12.

sentence
completions

SENTENCE COMPLETIONS ARE NOT ONLY ABOUT knowing vocabulary. Sentence Completions (which we call "SCs") are as much about understanding what's going on in the sentence as they are about knowing the vocab necessary to complete the blanks. In fact, if you know how to analyze the sentence surrounding the blank, you'll be able to figure out the answers without knowing the vocab at all. Showing you how to do that is what this chapter is all about.

SENTENCE COMPLETION INSTRUCTIONS

Read and learn the instructions for SCs before you show up to take the test.

> Each sentence below has one or two blanks, each blank indicating that something has been omitted. Beneath the sentence are five words or sets of words labeled A through E. Choose the word or set of words that, when inserted in the sentence, <u>best</u> fits the meaning of the sentence as a whole.
>
> Example:
>
> Medieval kingdoms did not become constitutional republics overnight; on the contrary, the change was ----.
>
> (A) unpopular
> (B) unexpected
> (C) advantageous
> (D) sufficient
> (E) gradual
>
> Correct Answer: E

WHAT THE INSTRUCTIONS *DON'T* SAY

The directions for SCs are pretty clear. You need to read a sentence and select the answer choice that *best* completes the sentence. That means you need to find the answer choice that is the best of all the possible choices, not just an answer choice that *can* complete the sentence.

The SC directions do include a mention of that subtle, yet crucial, fact, but they leave out three other key facts. Here are the three key facts and why you need to know them:

KEY FACT	WHAT IT IS	WHY IT'S IMPORTANT
1	Almost every SC contains all the information you need to define the word that fits in the blank.	You can use the context of the sentence to figure out what the missing words mean. You don't need to look at the answer choices first.
2	Every answer choice makes the sentence grammatically correct.	You won't be able to look at grammar to try to figure out the right answer. Only meaning matters.
3	SCs appear in order of difficulty within a timed section. The first third is easy, the second third moderately difficult, and the last third difficult.	If a question is easy or moderate, you can usually trust your first instincts. If you're on a difficult question, take a second to look out for SAT trickery before moving on.

HOW SCS WORK: A BUNCH OF PARTS

Every sentence is built out of a bunch of parts. The most important parts you need to know to beat SCs are **clauses** and **conjunctions**.

- **Clauses**: The parts of a sentence that contain a noun and a verb. Every complete sentence must contain at least one clause, and every clause should convey one idea. SCs always present you with *compound sentences*, which means they contain more than one clause. In compound sentences, clauses can either support or contrast each other. Clauses that support each other contain a consistent flow of ideas with no opposition within the sentence. For example, this sentence contains two clauses that support each other: "The test was easy, so I aced it." Clauses that contrast each other contain a flow of ideas that oppose each other. For example, this sentence contains clauses that contrast each other: "The test was easy, but I failed it."

- **Conjunctions**: Words that join clauses, like *so* and *but* in the previous examples, are called *conjunctions*. Conjunctions are important on SC questions because they often reveal how a sentence's clauses relate to each other. Knowing how clauses relate enables you to determine what kind of word(s) you need to fill in the blanks. In the sentence, "The test was easy, but I failed it," the conjunction *but* indicates that the two clauses *contrast*— although you would expect that the writer of this sentence would pass an easy test, the conjunction *but* signals a contrast, which sets up the unexpected idea that the writer of this sentence failed the test.

SC Electricity

One of the simplest ways to understand how sentences work is to imagine them as electrical ciruits. Let's talk very basic electricity for a few minutes.

Here's how electricity works: An electric current flows along a path called a circuit, which carries the current from one point to another. Along the way, switches at certain key points of the circuit tell the current which way the flow should go.

Think of every sentence as a circuit. The clauses are the current and the conjunctions are the switches that direct the flow of the sentence.

- sentence = circuit
- clauses = current
- conjunctions = switches

Some sentences flow in one direction from start to finish. An example of a sentence in which the clauses flow one way is, "Sarah slept until noon and was wired all night." The two clauses, *Sarah slept until noon* and *was wired all night*, are joined by the conjunction *and*, a switch that tells you that the two clauses *support* each other. If someone sleeps until noon, you'd expect them to be wired all night; the *and* in this sentence signals that you're expectations will be met.

Other conjunctions signal a *contrast* between the clauses that make up a sentence. For example, in the sentence, "Sarah slept until noon but was still tired by nine p.m.," the conjunction *but* serves as a switch that signals a contrast, or opposition, between the two clauses in the sentence. You'd expect that Sarah would have trouble falling asleep, since she slept until noon; that *but* signals that you're expectations will *not* be met in this case.

SCS: A FIVE-STEP METHOD

We've developed a five-step method based on our electricity model to help you find the answer choice that best fills in the blank(s).

Here are the five steps, complete with an explanation of each:

Step 1. Spot the Switch
Step 2. Go with the Flow
Step 3. Fill in the Blank
Step 4. Compare Your Answer to the Answer Choices
Step 5. Plug It In

Step 1: Spot the Switch

As we discussed, every electrical current flows along a path with one or more switches that direct which way the flow goes. Most SC sentences contain conjunction words that function like switches, pointing the meaning of the sentence in different directions. Some examples of these words include *so, however, thus,* and *although*. We call these words "switches."

The first thing you should do on every SC you come across is search for the switch. Not every sentence contains a switch, but many do. To make switch-spotting as easy as possible, here is a list of the switch words that most commonly appear on the SAT. There are two types of switches: one-way and two-way:

One-Way Switches

and	because	since	so	therefore	thus

Two-Way Switches

although	but	despite	however	instead	nevertheless
notwithstanding		rather	though	unless	while

Step 2: Go with the Flow

Every switch word can tell you which way the flow of the sentence goes. A one-way switch points out a one-way sentence. A two-way switch points out a two-way sentence.

- **One-way sentences** contain no contrast, which means they <u>flow in one direction</u>. All parts of the sentence support the main idea of the sentence.
- **Two-way sentences** contain a <u>break in the flow of the sentence that makes one part of the sentence contrast with another part</u>. Often the contrast comes after a comma or semicolon that divides the sentence.

Examples will make all of this much easier to see and understand.

One-Way Switches

Here's an example of an SC question that contains a one-way switch. Try to pick out the switch on your own before you read the explanation that follows.

> Since the scientist's years of research finally confirmed his theories, everyone ---- him.

The switch in this sentence is *since*. It's a one-way switch, so it tells you that the sentence's flow goes one way. And knowing that the sentence is one-way allows you to figure out how the sentence works.

The part of the sentence before the comma says that a scientist did a ton of research that finally confirmed his original theories. The part after the comma, which contains the blank, describes the reaction to the scientist's research and theories. Because the sentence is one-way, the word in the blank must *support* the idea that the scientist's years of hard work have finally paid off.

Now that you've used the rest of the sentence to clue you into what the blank might mean, you can begin to come up with your own possible answers to fill in the blank. Ask yourself what people would do in that circumstance? They'd probably do something like *congratulate* or *cheer* the scientist *since* his research paid off, right? Exactly.

Two-Way Switches

A two-way switch indicates that the sentence contains a contrast and therefore flows two ways. Here's an almost identical version of the sentence you just saw. Only one word has been changed.

something bad because of

Although the scientist's years of research finally confirmed his theories, everyone ---- him.

Once you've spotted the switch word *although*, you can use it to determine how the blank goes with the flow. The two-way switch word *although* indicates a *contrast*, so the blank must not support the idea of the scientist's research finally paying off. Once you've figured out which way the flow goes, you need to find the answer choice that goes with the flow of the sentence. Rather than *cheer* or *congratulate* the scientist, in this version of the sentence everyone must do something like *criticize* or *reject* the scientist.

No Switches

Not *every* sentence contains a switch. But whether there's a switch in a sentence or not, it's still vital that you figure out if the sentence flows one way or two ways.

And, luckily enough, there's a simple rule about sentences that don't have any switch words:

- A sentence without a switch will be one-way unless that sentence describes a change over time.

Sentences Describing a Change Over Time

There's one type of sentence that doesn't contain a switch word but can still flow two ways. These are sentences that compare two different periods of time. For example,

good because of a dramatic switch

Once a ---- movie director, Mickey Carson ended his life a pauper unable to finance the making of his own films.

Though this sentence does not contain a switch, it contains a two-way flow because it conveys an unexpected change over time. The main idea of the sentence focuses on a contrast: that Mickey Carson died a pauper even though he was once a ---- movie director. Words that you might come up with to go with the two-way flow of the sentence may include *successful, rich, celebrated*—all adjectives that contrast with the idea of a movie director who died in poverty.

If you can't find a switch word in a sentence, first check to see if the sentence describes a change over time. If it does, you've got a two-way sentence. If it doesn't, you've got a one-way sentence. Once you've determined that, come up with words that go with the flow as we just did in the previous example.

Following the Flow

On all SCs, if the sentence flows one way, ask yourself what main idea of the sentence the blank must *support*. If the sentence flows two ways, ask yourself which idea the blank must *contrast*. Here are some examples to test your ability to pick out the switch, follow the flow, and figure out which answer choices go with the flow.

> Despite the violently harsh weather conditions, the hikers ---- and made it back to their base camp.

[handwritten: good + contrast, old age]

What's the switch?	*despite*
Which way does the flow go?	two ways
What idea does the blank support or contrast?	contrasts with "the violently harsh weather conditions"

In this sentence, the switch word *despite* makes it clear that whatever fits into the blank has to contrast with the "violently harsh weather conditions." That means the sentence flows two ways. Now ask yourself what kind of word would go with the flow. The switch word *despite* tells you that there's a contrast in the sentence, which means the campers do make it back despite the harsh weather. Ask yourself what the campers would have to do to make it back despite threatening weather. They would have to *endure* or *survive*, right? That's the kind of word you would need to find among the answer choices.

Now try this example:

[handwritten: learned something that follows, so]

> Alex grew up near the beach, <u>so</u> he ---- how to surf at a very young age.

What's the switch?	*so*
Which way does the flow go?	one way
What idea does the blank support or contrast?	supports "grew up near the beach"

The switch word *so* in this example indicates that the sentence flows one way. That means all parts of the sentence must support the ideas that the sentence expresses. The word that fills in the blank must fit with the common conception of people who grow up by the beach. Ask yourself what their relationship to surfing would be at a young age. Would they learn to surf at a young age? Or know about surfing at a young age? Probably. That means you need to look for words like *learned* and *knew* in the answer choices. That would make the completed sentence read something like, *Alex grew up near the beach, so he learned how to surf at a very young age.*

Step 3: Fill in the Blank

You might have noticed that we haven't included the answer choices in our examples. We did that by design. Why?

Because you should try to come up with your own answer to fill in the blank or blanks in an SC *before* looking at the answer choices. That way you won't fall prey to SAT traps that the test may have planted among the answer choices. Coming up with your own answer first will also force you to stick with step 1 and step 2, which will prevent you from speeding along and making careless errors.

The answer that you generate to fill in the blank or blanks can be either a single word or a quick description of the type of word that you think should go in the blank.

Let's go back to a previous example, now with answer choices.

> Despite the violently harsh weather conditions, the hikers ---- and made it back to their base camp.
>
> (A)   surrendered
> (B)   won
> (C)   succeeded
> (D)   collapsed
> (E)   evacuated

What's the switch?	*despite*
Which way does the flow go?	two ways
What idea does the blank support or contrast?	contrasts with "the violently harsh weather conditions"

In step 2, we determined that the switch word *despite* indicates that the sentence flows two ways. That means the word in the blank must contrast with the idea of the violently harsh weather conditions. Ask yourself what the hikers would have to do despite the violently harsh weather conditions to make it back to camp. What word pops into your head? *Managed*? *Survived*? *Endured*? All of those choices are great. They go with the flow of the sentence and convey the idea of the hikers making it back despite the harsh weather. Now on to step 4.

Step 4: Compare Your Answer to the Answer Choices

Once you've used the information in the sentence to build your own answer, *then* you should go to the answer choices and look for a choice that matches yours.

In the example about the hikers, you can throw out *surrendered, collapsed,* and *evacuated,* because none of them even come close to your own answers.

That leaves you to choose between *succeeded* and *won*. Which is the better answer? Step 5 will help determine that.

Step 5: Plug It In

When you've got a new electrical device like a microwave or a TV, there's only one way to test whether it works: Plug it in. Same goes for testing out answer choices on *all* SCs. Always plug in the answer choice (or choices) you've selected to make sure your choice works in the sentence.

In the last example, we were trying to decide between *won* and *succeeded*. Plug both words in to determine which one fits *best* into the sentence.

> Despite the violently harsh weather conditions, the hikers *won* and made it back to their base camp.

> Despite the violently harsh weather conditions, the hikers *succeeded* and made it back to their base camp.

After plugging the two words in, *succeeded* seems like the better choice. The hikers weren't playing a game or involved in an contest, so the idea of having *won* something is inappropriate here.

You probably didn't have much trouble deciding between *won* and *succeeded* in this example. You may even be thinking that this plugging in step is a waste of time. It's not. Never skip step 5. Always plug in to check your answer choice.

IF VOCAB'S GOT YOU DOWN

Sentence Completions aren't all about vocab. But they are *somewhat* about vocab. And if you don't know the words huddling in those answer choices, things can get tough. But there *are* ways to attack SCs even if you don't know what all the words in the answer choices mean.

In fact, the first few steps for handling SCs with tough vocab are exactly the same as those for SCs with vocab you know:

1. Spot the Switch
2. Go with the Flow
3. Fill in the Blank

If you follow our five-step method, you shouldn't even look at the answer choices until after you've gone through the first three steps and figured out your own answer or phrase to fill in the blank. By ignoring the answer choices at first and instead focusing on the sentence, you eliminate the possibility that you'll be intimidated by hard vocabulary. This is important because it's *always* worthwhile to at least try to answer each SC. Why? Because once you've analyzed the sentence and have your own answer to fill the blank, it becomes much easier to eliminate answer choices, even if you don't completely know what they mean.

So, let's say you've gone through the first three steps. You've spotted the switches, if there are any. You've figured out the flow and how the blank fits into it. You've come up with your own answer. Then you go to the answer choices and realize you don't really know what they mean. What do you do? What tool can possibly save you from this mess? Word Charge.

Word Charge

Sentence Completion vocab words can often be broken down into one of two categories: positive or negative. That's "Word Charge." Nice happy words have a positive charge; dark unhappy words have a negative charge.

Word Charge is important on SCs for two reasons:

1. The Word Charge of the blank and the word that fills the blank must be the same. For example, a negative answer choice can never fill a blank that needs a positive word.
2. Even when you don't know the exact meaning of a word, you'll often have a sense of its "charge."

These two reasons add up to one great big fact: You can use Word Charge to sort through SC answer choices with tough vocab even if you don't know the exact meaning of the words. Below is a list of tough words to give you a chance to test out your sense of Word Charge. Cover up the column all the way on the right and try to guess each word's charge.

Word	Your Guess at Its Charge	Actual Charge
insidious	negitive	negative
diabolical	negitive	negative
effervescent	positive	positive
truculent	negitive	negative
vivacious	negitive	Positive

Finding Word Charge: Word Roots

English has been developing as a language for a long time. It keeps getting bigger and bigger and adding new words. New words are made out of old words or out of parts of old words. These building blocks are called *word roots*. When you're looking for the Word Charge of a word you don't know, look within the word for roots of other words whose meanings you *do* know. The best place to look for word roots is in the *prefix*—the first 1 to 5 letters of a word.

Different roots have different basic meanings. For example, take the word *disconsolate*. You might not know this word. But you probably *do* have an idea of what the word *consolation* means. Ever heard of a "consolation prize"? That's the prize that game shows give to the losers. It's usually a board game of the show they're on or a gift certificate for a haircut. It's meant to *console* them for losing.

Even if you don't know the word *consolation*, you might know the word *console*, which lies at the root of the big scary word *disconsolate*. *Console* means to provide comfort in a time of sorrow or loss. The prefix *dis-* before *-consolate* means *not*. Put it all together and you can make a solid guess that *disconsolate* means "not consoled" or "grieving due to loss."

Learning even just a few key building blocks of words and what they mean can be extremely helpful in determining Word Charge. We provide a list of word roots that most commonly appear in SAT vocab in our chapter on new SAT Vocab (page 135).

Word Charge in Action

Okay, enough explanation. Time for an example:

> The East Coast Hamstaz was a terrible rap group in the early '90s; its music was dull and its lyrics ----.
>
> (A)   grandiloquent
> (B)   magnanimous
> (C)   truculent
> (D)   fatuous
> (E)   trenchant

Now answer this question step by step using our five-step SC method.

1. Spot the Switch

This sentence does not contain a switch. There's no word in the sentence that signals that the blank must support or contrast with the main ideas expressed in the sentence.

2. Go with the Flow

So, there's no switch, and a quick read-through of the sentence shows that it isn't about a change over time. This sentence must therefore flow one-way. The blank, which describes the Hamstaz lyrics, must therefore support the other ideas in the sentence:

What's the switch?	none
Which way does the flow go?	one way
What idea does the blank support or contrast?	supports "The East Coast Hamstaz was a terrible rap group"

3. Fill in the Blank

Now you know that the blank, which describes the lyrics of the rap group, supports the idea of the East Coast Hamstaz being a terrible rap group. Ask yourself: "Self, what must the lyrics of the Hamstaz have been like if the Hamstaz were a terrible rap group?" The lyrics must have been *bad*.

> The East Coast Hamstaz was a terrible rap and R&B group in the early '90s; its music was dull and its lyrics *bad*.

4. Compare Your Answer to the Answer Choices

So far, you've breezed through this one. Time to take a look at the answer choices and find the one that matches up with *bad*.

> (A)   grandiloquent
> (B)   magnanimous
> (C)   truculent
> (D)   fatuous
> (E)   trenchant

What the . . . ? Which of these tough vocab words matches up with *bad*? Okay, keep cool. Don't give up just because the answer choices are filled with difficult vocabulary. Instead, use Word Charge.

In fact, you've already begun the Word Charge process. When you came up with your own answer for the blank in step 3, you also came up with the charge for the blank. The word that you thought should fill the blank was *bad*, which has a negative charge. That means you already know you need to find a negative word among the answer choices.

Take a run down the list and try to cut words that you think are positive based on their word roots or other clues you can decipher. Let's see: **A**, *grandiloquent*, sounds like a combination of *grand* and *eloquent*, both positive words. Cut it. **B**, *magnanimous*, sounds like "magnificent." Cut **B** too. Let's say that's as far as you can get with Word Charge. Stop there, and take a look at how far you've come.

By eliminating two answer choices, you've tipped the guessing odds strongly in your favor, without knowing the meaning of *any* of the answer choices. Sos the moral of the Word Charge story is, Word Charge may not always get you the correct answer, but it will help your score by making you a better guesser.

5. Plug It In

The last step is always to test-drive your answer choice by plugging it back in to the original sentence. In this example, you've used Word Charge to eliminate two answers, leaving you with three that seem to have the negative charge you need:

> The East Coast Hamstaz was a terrible rap and R&B group in the early '90s; its music was dull and its lyrics *bad*.
>
> (A)   grandiloquent (CUT)
> (B)   magnanimous (CUT)
> (C)   truculent
> (D)   fatuous
> (E)   trenchant

When you're faced with three words with charges you think you know, but with meanings you don't know at all, plugging in won't help. If that's the case, as in this example, the best thing you can do is pick any remaining answer immediately knowing that you've used Word Charge to tip the guessing odds in your favor. When you do have a sense of what the words mean, plug the answer you think is best back into the sentence to make sure it works. The correct answer to this question is **D**, fatuous, which means weak, silly, or foolish.

PRACTICE THE PROCESS

The best way to get the five-step SC process down cold is to practice. To that end, we give you examples of every type of SC under the sun: one-blankers, two-blankers, one-way, two-way, every single possible combination.

There are four different types of SCs.

1.   **One-Blank/One-Way**
2.   **One-Blank/Two-Way**
3.   **Two-Blank/One-Way**
4.   **Two-Blank/Two-Way**

Through the rest of this chapter we give you examples of each type, sometimes more than one. We then work out each example according to our five-step process.

SC Type 1: One-Blank/One-Way

About a third of the SAT SCs are one-blank/one-way. That's good news. They're the simplest type. Because the flow is one way, the blank will agree with the rest of the sentence. One-blank/one-way SCs almost never contain switch words.

There are two basic one-blank/one-way varieties:

- A **simple sentence** with no switch and with one missing word.
- A **compound sentence** with two halves split by a semicolon, colon, or comma. Usually, the first half of these SCs contains the blank, and the second half describes the word that goes in the blank.

Want some examples of what these actually look like? You got 'em.

Example: Simple Sentence

> The ---- waves in Maui terrified the surfers.

1. Spot the Switch
This sentence contains no switch and isn't about a change over time, so it must be one-way.

2. Go with the Flow
Since the sentence is one-way, the blank must agree with the rest of the sentence. Well, what's the blank about? It refers to the size of the waves. Meanwhile, the rest of the sentence refers to the fact that the waves terrified the surfers.

What's the switch?	none
Which way does the flow go?	one way
What idea does the blank support or contrast?	Supports "waves that terrify the surfers"

3. Fill in the Blank
You know that the waves have to be the kind of waves that could terrify the surfers. What kind of waves could do that? How about *really big* waves.

> The *really big* waves in Maui terrified the surfers.

4. Compare Your Answer to the Answer Choices
Now go to the answer choices and find the one that matches up with the answer you created just from looking at the sentence.

> (A)   slight
> (B)   gentle
> (C)   tremendous
> (D)   rolling
> (E)   salty

The answer that seems to match *really big* best is **C**, *tremendous*.

5. Plug It In
The last step. Plug the choice you think is the answer back into the sentence.

> The *tremendous* waves in Maui terrified the surfers.

Works perfectly. You're done.

Example: Compound Sentence with a Colon

> Employees were constantly amazed by the CEO's ---- speeches: She seemed unable to put together a coherent sentence.

1. Spot the Switch
This sentence contains no switch and isn't about a change over time, so it must be one-way.

2. Go with the Flow
Since the sentence is one way, the blank must agree with the rest of the sentence. What's the blank about? It describes the CEO's speeches. The rest of the sentence also describes the speeches by saying that the CEO "seemed unable to put together a coherent sentence."

What's the switch?	none
Which way does the flow go?	one way

3. Fill in the Blank

Since the sentence is one way, you know that the blank describing the CEO's speeches must support the idea that she can't put together a coherent sentence. In other words, the CEO's speeches must be *bad*.

Employees were constantly amazed by the CEO's *bad* speeches: She seemed unable to put together a coherent sentence.

4. Compare Your Answer to the Answer Choices

Now go to the answer choices and find the one that matches up with the answer you created just from looking at the sentence.

(A)   excellent
(B)   voluminous
(C)   inarticulate
(D)   timid
(E)   efficient

So, the CEO's speeches are *bad*. Which words in the answer choices fit the idea of a *bad* speech? **A** and **E** don't. They're positive words. *Voluminous* means big (based on the root "volume"). Cut *voluminous*. That leaves *timid* and *inarticulate*. Both of those words are negative, but *inarticulate* is specifically used for describing a bad speaker. So, inarticulate seems like the best answer.

Even if you didn't know the vocab, you still should have been able to use Word Charge to eliminate one, two, or even three of the answer choices.

5. Plug It In

The last step. Plug the choice you think is the answer back into the sentence.

Employees were constantly amazed by the CEO's *inarticulate* speeches: She seemed unable to put together a coherent sentence.

Example: Compound Sentence with a Comma

Many people consider the team ----, unmatched in skill or determination by any other team in the league.

1. Spot the Switch

This sentence contains no switch and isn't about a change over time, so it must be one-way.

2. Go with the Flow

Since the sentence is one-way, the blank must agree with the rest of the sentence. What's the blank about? How the team is perceived. The rest of the sentence also describes how the team is perceived—as "unmatched in skill or determination."

What's the switch?	none
Which way does the flow go?	one way
Which idea does the blank support or contrast?	supports "unmatched in skill or determination"

3. Fill in the Blank

Since the sentence is one-way, you know that the blank describing the team must fit with the fact that many people believe that the team is "unmatched in skill or determination." In other words, Hector must be *extremely good*.

> Many people consider the team *extremely good*, unmatched in skill or determination by any other team in the league.

4. Compare Your Answer to the Answer Choices
Now go to the answer choices and find the one that matches up with the answer you created just from looking at the sentence.

> (A)   middling
> (B)   destructive
> (C)   artistic
> (D)   quiescent
> (E)   invincible

You're looking for an answer choice that fits with the phrase *extremely good*, a very positive word. You should be able to eliminate *middling*, since it contains the root *middle*, which is the embodiment of average. You should also be able to eliminate *destructive*, since it's a negative term. That leaves *artistic*, *quiescent*, and *invincible*. *Artistic* is a positive term but has little to do with team sports, the subject of the sentence. *Quiescent* means "quiet and calm," which also does not fit with the sports theme of the sentence. That leaves *invincible*, which means "cannot be defeated," a perfect fit for the idea of an *extremely good* team.

Once again, even if you didn't know all the vocab words, you could have cut several answers using Word Charge, putting you in a stronger position to guess.

5. Plug It In
Plug the choice you think is the answer back into the sentence.

> Many people consider the team *invincible*, unmatched in skill or determination by any other team in the league.

This five-step method is quickly making you invincible.

SC Type 2: One-Blank/Two-Way
On these SCs, the blank *contrasts* with the main idea of another clause in the sentence. Most one-blank/two-way sentences contain a switch that signals the contrast in the sentence. A few examples that convey a change over time will *not* contain a switch. We provide examples of both.

One-Blank/Two-Way with Switch

> Christina considered her pranks ----, but her former friends found her actions annoying and juvenile.

1. Spot the Switch
This sentence contains the two-way switch *but*. That means it must be two-way.

2. Go with the Flow
Since the sentence is two-way, the blank must contrast with the main ideas expressed in the rest of the sentence. The rest of the sentence describes how other people found Christina's pranks "annoying and juvenile." That means Christina's view of her pranks must contrast or oppose that perspective.

What's the switch?	*but*
Which way does the flow go?	two ways

What idea does the blank support or contrast?	contrasts "her pranks were annoying and juvenile"

3. Fill in the Blank

Since the sentence is two-way, you know that the blank describing Christina's view of her pranks must contrast with the common view of her actions, which is that they were "annoying and juvenile." So, to contrast "annoying and juvenile," maybe Christina thinks that her pranks are *funny and playful*.

> Christina thought her pranks were *funny and playful*, but her former friends found her actions annoying and juvenile.

4. Compare Your Answer to the Answer Choices

Now go to the answer choices and find which one of them matches up with the answer you created just from looking at the sentence.

> (A)   hilarious
> (B)   angry
> (C)   colossal
> (D)   trite
> (E)   new

You're looking for an answer choice that fits with the phrase *funny and playful*, which is positive. You should be able to eliminate *angry* and *trite* ("corny"), since those are both negative. That leaves *hilarious, colossal,* and *new. Hilarious* is positive and means "extremely funny," so it's a very strong choice. *Colossal* has the same root as *colossus* and means "very big." It doesn't make much sense in a sentence that's about pranks or as a contrast to "annoying and juvenile." *New* is a positive word, but it also doesn't make sense as a contrast to "annoying and juvenile." *Hilarious* is the best choice.

Even if you didn't know all the vocab words, you should at least have been able to eliminate *angry* through Word Charge and *new* through the context of the sentence.

5. Plug It In

Plug the choice you think is the answer back into the sentence.

> Christina thought her pranks were *hilarious*, but her former friends found her actions annoying and juvenile.

One-Blank/Two-Way with No Switch

> Once a(n) ---- theory, the notion that the earth revolves around the sun is now accepted by virtually everyone.

1. Spot the Switch

This sentence contains no switch. However, the sentence does describe a change over time. Remember: Change-over-time sentences flow two ways even though they contain no switch.

2. Go with the Flow

Since the sentence is two-way, the blank must contrast with the ideas expressed in the rest of the sentence. The rest of the sentence describes how the idea of the earth revolving around the sun is accepted now "by virtually everyone." That means the blank must contrast with, or oppose, the idea that the earth revolving around the sun is widely accepted.

What's the switch?	none (change over time)
Which way does the flow go?	two ways
What idea does the blank support or contrast?	contrasts "accepted by virtually everyone"

3. Fill in the blank

Since the sentence is two-way, you know that the blank describing the old view of the theory must contrast with the current widespread acceptance of it. Previously, the theory must have been *not believed*.

> Once a(n) *not believed* theory, the notion that the earth revolves around the sun is now accepted by virtually everyone.

4. Compare Your Answer to the Answer Choices

Now go to the answer choices and find the one that matches up with the answer you created just from looking at the sentence.

(A)	terrific
(B)	pleasant
(C)	esteemed
(D)	beloved
(E)	controversial

You're looking for an answer choice that fits with the phrase *not believed*, which is negative. Go down the list. *Terrific* is positive. So is *pleasant*, *esteemed*, and *beloved*. So *controversial* must be the answer. And it is.

You should note, though, that *not believed* and *controversial* really don't mean the same thing. Something that is controversial is believed by some people and not by others. That's the definition of a controversy: It's an argument between two passionate sides. Here's the lesson to learn from this example: When you make up your own answer, you should be flexible with it. If you find an answer choice that matches it exactly, awesome. If you don't, look for an answer choice that matches your answer's Word Charge and fits the context of the sentence.

5. Plug It In

Plug the choice you think is the answer back into the sentence.

> Once a(n) *controversial* theory, the notion that the earth revolves around the sun is now accepted by virtually everyone.

SC Type 3: Two-Blank/One-Way

Two-blank/one-way sentences sometimes contain switches like *and*, *because*, *since*, *so*, and *therefore*. Many two-blank/one-way sentences don't contain any switch at all.

Two-blank/one-way sentences come in two basic forms: blanks close together and blanks far apart. With blanks close together, you need to look at the half of the sentence that does not contain the blanks; with blanks far apart, you need to use clues from both halves of the sentence. That's the key difference between the two kinds of two-blank/one-way SCs.

Also note that with two-blank sentences, you have to take into account how *both* blanks function in the sentence when you're working on step 2.

Blanks Close Together

> The ---- conditions ---- even the intrepid explorer, who never again ventured out into the tundra.

1. Spot the Switch

This sentence contains no switch word and doesn't describe a change over time. That means it's one-way.

2. Go with the Flow

Since the sentence is one-way, both blanks must support the ideas expressed in the rest of the sentence. The rest of the sentence describes the explorer as intrepid and then says that even the explorer never again ventured into the tundra. That means the first blank must describe conditions that would convince even a bold explorer never to venture out again.

What's the switch?	none
Which way does the flow go?	one way
What idea does the blank support or contrast?	supports "even the intrepid explorer never went into the tundra again"

The second blank describes what the conditions did to the explorer to convince him never to venture out into the tundra again.

What's the switch?	none
Which way does the flow go?	one way
What idea does the blank support or contrast?	supports "even the intrepid explorer never went into the tundra again"

3. Fill in the Blank

Since the sentence is two-way, you know that the blanks describing the conditions and what happened to the intrepid explorer must agree with the fact that he never again went out into the tundra. Would the explorer have refused to go back into the tundra if the conditions were nice? That wouldn't make sense. The conditions most have been *terrible*. And what would terrible conditions have done to the explorer? *Scared* him, or perhaps even *injured* him.

> The *terrible* conditions *scared* even the intrepid explorer, and he never again ventured out into the tundra.

4. Compare Your Answer to the Answer Choices

Now go to the answer choices and find the one that matches up with the answer you created just from looking at the sentence.

> (A)   destructive..angered
> (B)   gorgeous..moved
> (C)   harsh..terrified
> (D)   appalling..enveloped
> (E)   serene..pleased

You're looking for two answer choices that fit with the words *terrible* and *scared*, both of which are negative. By Word Charge, you should be able to eliminate **B**, **D**, and **E**, since each of those pairs of words contains at least one word that's positive. Between **A**, *destructive..angered*, and **C**, *harsh..terrified*, answer **C** seems much stronger, since *terrified* is such a close fit with *scared*.

5. Plug It In

Plug the choice you think is the answer back into the sentence.

> The *harsh* conditions *terrified* even the intrepid explorer, and he never again ventured out into the tundra.

Blanks Far Apart

> Clarence Eichen was a ---- musician from a very young age, and he became the most ---- tuba performer in the world during the 1980s.

1. Spot the Switch

This sentence contains the one-way switch *and*. It must be one-way.

2. Go with the Flow

Since the sentence is one-way, both blanks must agree with the rest of the sentence. The rest of the sentence describes what sort of musician Eichen became. The first blank is about Eichen being a musician at a very young age.

What's the switch?	*and*
Which way does the flow go?	one way
What idea does the blank support or contrast?	supports "became the most ---- in the world"

The second blank describes what sort of performer Clarence became as an adult. The rest of the sentence describes what sort of musician he was as a child.

What's the switch?	*and*
Which way does the flow go?	one way
What idea does the blank support or contrast?	supports "was a ---- musician from a young age"

3. Fill in the Blank

The interesting thing about this sentence is that the two blanks refer to each other. That may make the sentence seem difficult to solve, since each blank stops you from guessing whether the other should be positive or negative. But since the sentence is one-way, you already do know something about the two blanks. Either they're both positive, or they're both negative. Either he was great as a boy and great as a man, or he was bad as a boy and bad as a man.

> Clarence Eichen was a *great* musician from a very young age, and he became the most *wonderful* tuba performer in the world during the 1980s.

or

> Clarence Eichen was a *bad* musician from a very young age, and he became the most *awful* tuba performer in the world during the 1980s.

4. Compare Your Answer to the Answer Choices

Now go to the answer choices and find the one that matches up with the answer you created just from looking at the sentence.

(A)   composed..tremulous
(B)   famous..accomplished
(C)   rigid..bellicose
(D)   calm..unstoppable
(E)   grave..humorous

None of the answer choices have two negatively charged pairs, so you don't have to worry about that. What you're looking for then, is a match for *great..wonderful*. You can eliminate **A**, **C**, and **E**, since *tremulous*, *rigid*, and *grave* all have negative charge. Now, does it make logical sense to call someone a *calm* musician? In most situations, it doesn't. So the best match for *great..wonderful* is *famous..accomplished*.

5. Plug It In

Plug the choice you think is the answer back into the sentence.

> Clarence Eichen was a *famous* musician from a very young age, and he became the most *accomplished* tuba performer in the world during the 1980s.

SC Type 4: Two-Blank/Two-Way

In two-blank/two-way SCs, one-half of the sentence flows against the other half. This two-way contrast is usually, but not always, marked by the presence of a two-way switch. Below are examples of two-blank/two-way SCs, with and without switches.

Two-Blank/Two-Way with Switch

> Faulkner's use of adjective-filled language in his novels is now admired as an inimitable aspect of his unique style and a product of his literary ----; when his fiction was first published, however, many critics often ---- his style as needlessly ornate.

1. Spot the Switch

This sentence contains the two-way switch *however*. That means it's two-way.

2. Go with the Flow

The sentence is two-way, and the blanks each appear in different halves of the sentence. Since it's a two-way sentence, the two blanks (and the parts of the sentence before and after the semicolon) must contrast each other.

The first blank relates to the source of Faulkner's "unique style" that is "now admired." The second blank describes the reaction of early critics of Faulkner who considered his style "needlessly ornate."

What's the switch?	*however*
Which way does the flow go?	two ways
What idea does the blank support or contrast?	contrasts "when his fiction was first published, critics ---- his style as needlessly ornate."

The second blank describes how the critics reacted to Faulkner's style. This is in contrast to modern critics who "admire" it.

What's the switch?	*however*
Which way does the flow go?	two ways
What idea does the blank support or contrast?	contrasts "Faulkner's style is now admired."

3. Fill in the Blank

Since the sentence is two-way, you know that the two blanks must contrast, or oppose, each other. The first half of the sentence tells us that critics now admire Faulkner's style, which means the word you need to fill the blank will likely have a positive Word Charge. If the critics admired Faulkner's style, what might they have identified as its source? His literary *what*? How about *talent*?

The second half of the sentence tells us that critics at first considered his literary style "needlessly ornate." This indicates that the blank should be filled with a word that has negative Word Charge. How about *criticized*?

> Faulkner's use of intense, adjective-filled language in his novels is now admired as an inimitable aspect of his unique style and a product of his literary *talent*; but when his fiction was first published, many critics often *criticized* his style as needlessly ornate.

4. Compare Your Answer to the Answer Choices

Now go to the answer choices and find the one that matches up with the answer you created just from looking at the sentence.

> (A)   proclivities..extolled
> (B)   discrimination..praised
> (C)   abilities..examined
> (D)   genius..decried
> (E)   bombast..enlightened

You're looking for one answer choice that fits with the words *talent* and *criticized*. The first word is positive, the second negative. You should be able to eliminate **B**, **C**, and **E**, because *praised*, *examined*, and *enlightened* are all relatively common vocab words that are positive, and you want the second word to be negative.

That leaves **A** and **D**. Deciding between these two is hard, particularly because three of the four words are very difficult vocab words. At worst, you should plug both choices back into the sentence and then guess which one sounds best. At best, you'd sense either that *genius* is more positive than *proclivities* or that *extolled* has a positive charge, either of which would mark **D** as the correct answer.

5. Plug It In
Plug the choice you think is the answer back into the sentence.

> Faulkner's use of intense, adjective-filled language in his novels is now admired as an inimitable aspect of his unique style and a product of his literary *genius*; but when his fiction was first published, many critics often *decried* his style as needlessly ornate.

Two-Blank/Two-Way with No Switch
Two-way sentences that do *not* contain a switch word will compare a change over time.

> Once considered bad for your ----, bathing is now thought to be a crucial way of maintaining the ---- conditions that prevent plagues and epidemics.

1. Spot the Switch
This sentence contains no switch, but it does compare a change over time. That means it's two-way.

2. Go with the Flow
The sentence is two-way, and the blanks are each in different halves of the sentence. That means that the two blanks must contrast with each other.

What's the first blank about? It states that people once considered bathing harmful. This contrasts with the second half of the sentence, which says that bathing is now thought to "prevent plagues and epidemics."

What's the switch?	none
Which way does the flow go?	two ways
What idea does the blank support or contrast?	contrasts with "prevent plagues and epidemics"

The second blank describes the "conditions" that "prevent plagues and epidemics." It contrasts with the first half of the sentence, which says that people once thought that bathing was "bad for your ----."

What's the switch?	none
Which way does the flow go?	two ways
What idea does the blank support or contrast?	contrasts with "bad for your ----".

3. Fill in the Blank

Since the sentence is two-way, you know that the two blanks must contrast each other. The blank in the first half of the sentence explains in what way people thought bathing could harm them. This blank is contrasted with the modern thought that bathing "prevents plagues and epidemics." In other words, modern people think bathing "protects health," while in earlier times, people thought bathing was *bad* for your health.

As for the second blank, it describes the conditions that "prevent plagues and epidemics" and contrasts with the idea that bathing harms health. How about bathing creates *healthy* conditions?

> Once considered bad for your *health*, bathing is now thought to be a crucial way of maintaining the *healthy* conditions that prevent plagues and epidemics.

4. Compare Your Answer to the Answer Choices

Now go to the answer choices and find the one that matches up with the answer you created just from looking at the sentence.

> (A) behavior..superb
> (B) relations..helpful
> (C) development..ideal
> (D) ethics..unfortunate
> (E) well-being..sanitary

You're looking for two answer choices that fit with the words *health* and *healthy*. A quick look through the answer choices shows one answer that stands out from the rest: **E**. *Well-being* and *sanitary* both fit with the idea of health and the need for positive words.

5. Plug It In

Plug the choice you think is the answer back into the sentence.

> Once considered bad for your *well-being*, bathing is now thought to be a crucial way of maintaining the *sanitary* conditions that prevent plagues and epidemics.

And that's it! You're now ready for any Sentence Completion that the new SAT might send your way. Following are some practice sets, with answers and explanations.

SENTENCE COMPLETIONS: PRACTICE SET 1

1. Despite harsh punishments for fugitive slaves and difficult journeys through the night, Harriet Tubman proved her strength in the years before the Civil War by ------- capture and ------- many slaves along the Underground Railroad.

   (A) avoiding . . barring
   (B) allowing . . advising
   (C) eluding . . guiding
   (D) disproving . . abandoning
   (E) choosing . . defending

2. Throughout the past decade, the turnip crop has been -------, sometimes yielding abundant harvests and sometimes offering only meager quantities.

   (A) unprecedented
   (B) illusory
   (C) temporary
   (D) unstable
   (E) impracticable

3. As a painter, Raoul needs to improve his ------- skills; his palette is often striking, but his forms seem ill-placed on the canvas.

   (A) remedial
   (B) compositional
   (C) deductive
   (D) mnemonic
   (E) intuitive

4. Although the erection of the Berlin Wall in 1961 had been carried out -------, with the East German government making no public announcement of its intention to seal the border, the wall's destruction in 1989 was ------- years earlier.

   (A) zealously . . impacted
   (B) warily . . acclaimed
   (C) openly . . concerned
   (D) hostilely . . approved
   (E) clandestinely . . foreseen

5. The press misunderstood the politician's remarks about the economy; instead of taking them as -------, as the politician intended, the press heard them as defeatist.

   (A) optimistic
   (B) regulatory
   (C) fiscal
   (D) reliable
   (E) indiscriminate

6. Although Rosa's apartment always seemed ------- to her guests, Rosa was not naturally -------
   and had to make a great effort to keep her home in order.

   (A) harmonious . . congenial
   (B) nondescript . . understated
   (C) immaculate . . fastidious
   (D) impressive . . generous
   (E) respectable . . vivacious

7. The advent of the compact disc in the 1980s relegated the vinyl record album to -------, making
   vinyl more important as a collectible than as a means of distributing new music.

   (A) perpetuity
   (B) obsolescence
   (C) success
   (D) renown
   (E) infamy

8. Last year, the president of the company donated ------- percentage of her income to charity, a
   shocking generosity unmatched among other executives of her stature.

   (A) an incompatible
   (B) a paltry
   (C) a monolithic
   (D) an exorbitant
   (E) an unspoken

9. The magnificent antique watch demonstrated both technical precision and aesthetic skill; the
   watchmaker obviously possessed a ------- talent.

   (A) prodigious
   (B) lamentable
   (C) quotidian
   (D) tenuous
   (E) normative

10. Before the Vietnam era, the American government had seemed beyond reproach, a virtual
    citadel of -------, but the war and events like Watergate helped to tarnish that image.

    (A) dubiety
    (B) languor
    (C) temerity
    (D) usurpation
    (E) rectitude

ANSWERS & EXPLANATIONS

1. **C**

The introductory clause, *despite harsh punishments for fugitive slaves and difficult journeys through the night*, clues you in to the core idea of this sentence: that something occurred in spite of these two things. Continuing, you run into Harriet Tubman, who *proved her strength* doing something with slaves despite the two obstacles mentioned in the first clause. What could she have done? *Despite harsh punishments* and *difficult journeys* play off *capture* and *along the Underground Railroad*. You can predict that Tubman managed to *avoid* the punishment and complete the journey.

Now you need to check out the answer choices to see which one fits your prediction. Let's start with *avoiding*. *Avoiding* certainly works; hang on to **A**. *Allowing* doesn't work; nix **B**. *Eluding* works; keep **C**. Neither *disproving* nor *choosing* works, so both **D** and **E** are out. At this point, if you're rushed, you can plug the second word in both **A** and **C** into the second blank and see which has a better ring to it. If you have the time, you can ask yourself, Does either *barring* or *guiding* match the idea that Tubman completed the journey? *Barring* does not, but *guiding* does. You should double-check now to be sure that **C** fits the sentence: *Despite harsh punishments for fugitive slaves and difficult journeys through the night, Harriet Tubman proved her strength in the years before the Civil War by eluding capture and guiding many slaves along the Underground Railroad.* **C** is correct.

In this case, if you predicted "avoiding," *avoiding* in **A** would immediately seem attractive. But always remember to check both words, since often one of the words fits while the other does not.

2.   **D**

Here, the main clause *the turnip crop has been ------* is followed by *sometimes yielding abundant harvests and sometimes offering only meager quantities*. So you know the blank must be filled by something indicating that the turnip crop is sometimes one way and sometimes another. You can predict that the blank will be filled with something meaning "unpredictable" or "changing."

Looking at the choices, *unprecedented* means "never seen before"; nix **A**. *Illusory* means "imaginary"; scratch **B**. *Temporary* means "not permanent." Is that the same as "changing" or "unpredictable"? Might be a close call, so hang on to **C**. *Unstable* means "tending to change." Is that a better fit than *temporary*? Yes, so keep **D** and eliminate **C**. *Impracticable* means "not capable of being done"; out with **E**. Now you need to read **D** back into the sentence: *Throughout the past decade, the turnip crop has been unstable, sometimes yielding abundant harvests and sometimes offering only meager quantities.* **D** works and is correct.

3.   **B**

The main clause, *Raoul needs to improve his ------ skills*, is followed by *his forms seem ill-placed on the canvas*. What you need is a word that describes the ability to arrange forms. You might not be able to come up with a single word off the top of your head, but you know the idea you're looking for.

Take a look at the choices. Does *remedial* have anything to do with arranging forms? No; it means "supplying a remedy." Eliminate **A**. Does *compositional* have anything to do with arranging forms? Yes; it means "having to do with composition," which is the arranging of forms. Keep **B**. *Deductive* means "based on reasoning," *mnemonic* means "related to memory," and *intuitive* means "based on a gut feeling." You can get rid of **C**, **D** and **E**. If you read **B** back into the sentence, you get: *As a painter, Raoul needs to improve his compositional skills; his palette is often striking, but his forms seem ill-placed on the canvas.* **B** works and is correct.

4.   **E**

The introductory clause says *Although the erection of the Berlin Wall in 1961 had been carried out ------* and is followed by a phrase indicating that the East German government said nothing about it. So we know the first blank will be filled by a word meaning "without public knowledge." The word *although* indicates that there will be a contrast in the sentence. So although no announcement had been made about the wall's erection, its *destruction in 1989 was ------ years earlier*. You need a word that will indicate that the destruction of the wall somehow contrasted with its secret construction. You can predict that the first word will mean "secret" and the second will mean "known."

Starting with "secret," scan the choices looking for a match. *Zealously* means "enthusiastically"; nix **A**. *Warily* means "cautiously"; get rid of **B**. *Openly* is the opposite of "secret," so eliminate **C**. *Hostilely* means "aggressively"; get rid of **D**. Does *clandestinely* mean "secret"? Yes. Even if you didn't know that already, the other choices don't work at all, so *clandestinely* must be the one. Read both words into the sentence: *Although the erection of the Berlin Wall in 1961 was carried out clandestinely, with the East German government making no public* announcement of its intention to seal the border, the wall's destruction in 1989 was foreseen years earlier*. Both words work: **E** is correct.

5. A

You know that the press *misunderstood the politician's remarks* and that they were taken as *defeatist* instead of what the politician intended. But what did the politician intend? The needed word will contrast with *defeatist*, which means "tending to expect defeat." So you need a word that means "tending to expect success."

Scanning the choices, *optimistic* means "anticipating the best possible outcome," so keep **A**. *Regulatory* means "relating to regulations"; scratch **B**. *Fiscal* means "relating to finances"; eliminate **C**. *Reliable* means "dependable"; get rid of **D**. *Indiscriminate* means "random"; eliminate **E**. The only choice that fits is *optimistic*: *The press misunderstood the politician's remarks about the economy; instead of taking them as optimistic, as the politician intended, the press heard them as defeatist*. **A** is correct.

6. C

The contrast here is indicated by *although*: *Although Rosa's apartment always seemed -------, Rosa was not naturally ------- and had to make a great effort to keep her home in order*. Both words here will contrast with *had to make a great effort to keep her home in order*. You know that Rosa is not naturally neat, even though her apartment always seems so. So you can predict that both words will be related to "neatness."

Scan the choices and compare each word to "neatness." Is *harmonious* related to "neatness"? No; eliminate **A**. Is *nondescript* related to "neatness"? No; eliminate **B**. Is *immaculate* related to "neatness"? Yes; keep **C**. Is *impressive* related to "neatness"? No; eliminate **D**. Is *respectable* related to "neatness"? Possibly, so keep **E**. You're down to **C** and **E**. Which is related to "neatness," *fastidious* or *vivacious*? *Fastidious* means "paying attention to detail" and *vivacious* means "lively." Of the two, *fastidious* is the better choice. Read **C** back into the sentence: *Although Rosa's apartment always seemed immaculate to her guests, Rosa was not naturally fastidious and had to make a great effort to keep her home in order*. **C** is correct.

7. B

The main clause says that the status of the vinyl album changed in the 1980s (*relegated the vinyl record album to -------*) and that it stopped being used as *a means of distributing new music*. You need a word that relates to the process of going from used to unused. It might be hard to come up with a single word right away, but keep the concept in mind when you scan the choices.

Does *perpetuity* relate to the process? No; *perpetuity* means "eternity." Eliminate **A**. Does *obsolescence* relate to the process? Yes; *obsolescence* means "the state of being outdated." Keep **B**. What about *success*, *renown*, and *infamy*? None of them is related to the process of becoming unused, so eliminate all three. Read **B** into the sentence: *The advent of the compact disc in the 1980s relegated the vinyl record album to obsolescence, making vinyl more important as a collectible than as a means of distributing new music*. **B** is correct.

8. D

The main clause of the sentence tells you that *the president of the company donated ------- percentage of her income to charity*. The following modifier adds that it was *a shocking generosity*. The word *shocking* is what you're trying to match here. You can predict that the correct answer will mean "shocking."

Does *incompatible* mean "shocking"? No; eliminate **A**. How about *paltry*? No; eliminate **B**. What about *monolithic*? This one might be tough, so hang on to it for a second. *Exorbitant*? That might work as well, so hang on to **D**, too. *Unspoken* doesn't mean "shocking," so nix it.

You're left with **C** and **D**. Read *monolithic* back into the sentence: *Last year, the president of the company donated a monolithic percentage of her income to charity, a shocking generosity unmatched among other executives of her stature.* Try *exorbitant*: *Last year, the president of the company donated an exorbitant percentage of her income to charity, a shocking generosity unmatched among other executives of her stature.* At this point you can use your ear and choose from the two for a 50/50 chance.

9. **A**

The second part of the sentence describes the watchmaker's talent. You know from the first part of the sentence that the watch was well-crafted. So you're looking for a word that praises the watchmaker's ability. Something that says he *possessed* "an enormous" *talent*. You can predict the correct answer will mean "enormous."

Prodigious means "impressively large," so keep **A**. *Lamentable* means "regrettable," so eliminate **B**. *Quotidian* means "commonplace"; eliminate **C**. *Tenuous* means "having little substance"; eliminate **D**. *Normative* means "relating to a standard"; eliminate **E**. **A** is the only choice whose meaning matches the prediction. Read **A** into the sentence: *The magnificent antique watch demonstrated both technical precision and aesthetic skill; the watchmaker obviously possessed a prodigious talent.* **A** is correct.

10. **E**

The main clause states that *the American government had seemed beyond reproach*, followed by the modifier *a virtual citadel of -------*. You need a word that plays off *beyond reproach*. *Reproach* means "criticism," so you're looking for *a citadel of* "something beyond criticism."

Turning to the choices, *dubiety* means "the state of being dubious"; eliminate **A**. *Languor* means "lack of energy"; eliminate **B**. *Temerity* means "a heedless disregard of danger"; eliminate **C**. *Usurpation* means "the act of seizing control"; eliminate **D**. *Rectitude* means "moral uprightness." That's a close match with "beyond criticism"; keep **E**. Read it into the sentence: *Before the Vietnam era, the American government had seemed beyond reproach, a virtual citadel of rectitude, but the war and events like Watergate helped to tarnish that image.* **E** is correct.

SENTENCE COMPLETIONS: PRACTICE SET 2

1. Although special effects have existed in cinema for decades, today's special effects engineers have access to ------- that would have ------- their counterparts in years past.

    (A) technology . . amazed
    (B) knowledge . . regaled
    (C) creativity . . altered
    (D) largesse . . instigated
    (E) profits . . amused

2. Driven by her competing desires to further her political vision and to pursue music, Joanna ------- her goals and became an activist folk singer.

    (A) refuted
    (B) combined
    (C) disallowed
    (D) gauged
    (E) conceded

3. The mathematician's proof was so ------- executed that her colleagues had to concede that it was -------, yet another example of her powerful insight.

    (A) faultlessly . . imprecise
    (B) hastily . . judicious
    (C) sporadically . . meticulous
    (D) cleverly . . brilliant
    (E) improperly . . disastrous

4. His supervisor's comments ------- Luis, causing him to feel awkward and embarrassed in front of his coworkers.

    (A) excited
    (B) mortified
    (C) rejuvenated
    (D) calmed
    (E) gladdened

5. Naomi wanted to save money, but she found being ------- difficult when there were still so many places she wanted to travel.

    (A) inflexible
    (B) lavish
    (C) dynamic
    (D) frugal
    (E) concise

6. As the year wore on, his study schedule, which was already -------, became so burdensome as to be completely -------.

   (A) beguiling . . uncontrollable
   (B) strenuous . . unmanageable
   (C) unproductive . . discordant
   (D) negligible . . purposeless
   (E) impractical . . superlative

7. Not content to offer his readers a ------- account of his life in politics, Winston Churchill ------- a deeply penetrating look at the inner workings of government.

   (A) meaningless . . disavows
   (B) facile . . provides
   (C) hurried . . constructs
   (D) precise . . promotes
   (E) capricious . . unveils

8. The food critic called the new restaurant -------, going so far as to describe it as -------; the menu, the service, and the décor had all been extraordinary.

   (A) mediocre . . pedestrian
   (B) preternatural . . déclassé
   (C) glorious . . moribund
   (D) irksome . . enervating
   (E) astounding . . sublime

9. There was no need to send food supplies to the village after the devastating floods; the storehouses had been spared and the villagers had a ------- of grain.

   (A) panoply
   (B) regalia
   (C) plethora
   (D) bastion
   (E) lacuna

ANSWERS & EXPLANATIONS

1. **A**

The main clause, *today's special effects engineers have access to ------- that would have ------- their counterparts in years past*, plays off the idea that *special effects have existed in cinema for decades*. So, despite the fact that movies have had these effects for years, today's special effects engineers have access to something new that previous generations of engineers would have reacted to in some way. Since the sentence deals with special effects, especially with the difference between old-timers and newcomers to the field, the first blank probably has something to do with the ability to create the effects. You can predict that the first blank will mean "methods."

If you scan the choices, *technology, knowledge,* and *creativity* could work, so keep **A**, **B**, and **C**. *Largesse* (meaning "generosity") and *profits* don't work, so eliminate **D** and **E**. Now you need to deal with the second word. Plug *amazed, regaled,* and *altered* into the sentence and use your ear to guide you to the best choice. Only *amazed* gives the sentence a clear, logical meaning: *Although special effects have existed in cinema for decades, today's special effects engineers have access to technology that would have amazed their counterparts in years past.* **A** is correct.

2. **B**

Here, you know that Joanna wanted *to further a liberal political vision and to pursue music.* You also know that she did something with those two goals and became an activist folk singer.

Since becoming an activist folk singer incorporates aspects of both her goals, you can predict that the blank will be filled by something meaning "merged."

Now you need to scan the choices, eliminating any words that don't convey the meaning of "merged." *Refuted* means "proved wrong"; eliminate **A**. *Combined* could work; keep **B**. *Disallowed* means "forbade"; eliminate **C**. *Gauged* means "measured"; eliminate **D**. *Conceded* means "to admit"; eliminate **E**. Plug **B** into the sentence: *Driven by her competing desires to further her political vision and to pursue music, Joanna combined her goals and became an activist folk singer*. **B** is correct.

3. **D**

The modifier *yet another example of her powerful insight* makes clear that the mathematician's proof was impressive. So you know you need to show that the proof was executed in such a way as to impress her colleagues. You can predict that the first word will mean "executed well" and the second "impressive."

Scanning the list for the first word, *faultlessly* and *cleverly* stand out, so keep **A** and **D**. The second words in the pairs, *imprecise* and *brilliant*, are pretty different, though. Which conveys the meaning of "impressive"? Only *brilliant*, so plug **D** into the sentence: *The mathematician's proof was so cleverly executed that her colleagues had to concede that it was brilliant, yet another example of her powerful insight*. **D** is correct.

4. **B**

At first, you know only that the supervisor's comments had some effect on Luis. As you continue reading, you see that they made him feel *awkward and embarrassed in front of his coworkers*. So the missing word must convey the meaning of "embarrass."

Scanning the choices, *excited*, *calmed*, and *gladdened* are relatively easy to eliminate, since none means "embarrass." Get rid of **A**, **C**, and **E**. What about *mortified* and *rejuvenate*? If you don't know their meanings exactly, plug each into the sentence and use your ear to pick the better choice. If you know that "to mortify" means "to shame or embarrass," then you can jump right to **B**: *His supervisor's comments mortified Luis, causing him to feel awkward and embarrassed in front of his coworkers*. **B** is correct.

5. **D**

The introductory clause tells you that Naomi wants to save money. The following clause tells you she thinks it's difficult to do so. You know you need a word that means "able to save money."

Inflexible doesn't mean "able to save money"; eliminate **A**. *Lavish*? If you're unsure, keep it for a moment. *Dynamic* doesn't mean "able to save money"; out with **C**. *Frugal*? Unsure? Keep it. *Concise* doesn't mean "able to save money," so eliminate **E**. We're left with **B** and **D**. Try plugging each into the sentence and see which sounds better. If you know the meaning of the words, you know that *lavish* and *frugal* are close to opposites. *Lavish* means "spending extravagantly." Not what you need. *Frugal* means "cautious with money." Plug it into the sentence: *Naomi wanted to save money, but she found being frugal difficult when there were still so many places she wanted to travel*. **D** is correct.

6. **B**

The sentence sets up a comparison between the study schedule at the beginning of the year and at the end. By the end it was *so burdensome as to be completely -------*. You know that the second word must mean something close to "burdensome."

Scanning the second word of each choice, *uncontrollable* in **A** and *unmanageable* in **B** stand out as possibilities. Keep them and eliminate the others. Now look at the first words of those two choices: *beguiling* and *strenuous*. Which is a better fit? We know that the study schedule had become even more of a burden than it *already* was, so we need a word that suggests "burdensome" again. Which is it? Try reading both choices into the sentence and see which sounds better. *As the year wore on, his study schedule, which was already strenuous, became so burdensome as to be completely unmanageable.* **B** is correct.

7.   B

The main clause *Winston Churchill ------- a deeply penetrating look at the inner workings of government* follows the modifier *Not content to offer his readers a ------- account of his life in politics.* So the contrast is between *deeply penetrating* and the blank in the modifier. You know the first word must be somewhat opposite to *deeply penetrating*, like "superficial."

Scanning the first words, *meaningless* and *facile* stand out as possibilities. Keep **A** and **B**. Eliminate the others. The second words in **A** and **B** are *disavows* and *provides. Disavows* means "to deny." Does that work in the sentence? Did Churchill deny *a deeply penetrating look...*? No; eliminate **A**. *Provides* parallels *offer* in the modifier. Read **B** into the sentence: *Not content to offer his readers a facile account of his life in politics, Winston Churchill provides a deeply penetrating look at the inner workings of government.* **B** is correct.

8.   E

The main clause states that the *critic called the new restaurant -------, going so far as to describe it as -------.* The second part of the sentence lets you know that the restaurant is top notch. So the critic must have called the restaurant "great" and gone so far as to describe it as "wonderful" or something like that. The phrase *going so far as to* is almost always a sign on the SAT that amplification is involved.

Scanning the choices, the only words in the first column that mean "great" are *glorious* in **C** and *astounding* in **E**. The second word in **C** is *moribund*, which means "on death's doorstep." **C** doesn't seem likely. The second word in **E**, *sublime*, continues the meaning and takes it up a notch. Sounds good so far. Read it into the sentence: *The food critic called the new restaurant astounding, going so far as to describe it as sublime; the menu, the service, and the décor had all been extraordinary.* **E** is correct.

9.   C

The first part of the sentence lets you know that the village did not need extra food after the flood. The second part, containing the blank, explains that *the storehouses had been spared* and that the villagers still had grain. The blank, then, must mean something like "enough" or "more than enough."

Panoply means "a shining array"; eliminate **A**. *Regalia* means "the symbols of a rank, office, order, or society"; eliminate **B**. *Plethora* means "an excess"; keep **C**. *Bastion* means "stronghold"; eliminate **D**. *Lacuna* means "gap or empty space"; eliminate **E**. The only one that works is **C**: *There was no need to send food supplies to the village after the devastating floods; the storehouses had been spared and the villagers had a plethora of grain.* **C** is correct.

SENTENCE COMPLETIONS: PRACTICE SET 3

1. The highway construction project required more funding than the state could -------, so the highway commission proposed working in ------- private sources.

    (A) demand . . opposition to
    (B) renege . . place of
    (C) review . . comparison with
    (D) justify . . harmony with
    (E) allocate . . association with

2. Reacting to reviews that called his work childish and -------, the artist began his next series of paintings with a determination to convey maturity and -------.

    (A) irresponsible . . sincerity
    (B) meaningless . . simplicity
    (C) vulgar . . refinement
    (D) tedious . . generosity
    (E) obscure . . decisiveness

3. Siberian tigers are considered among the most ------- of animals; their striking coloration, powerful musculature, and aloof bearing leave many people -------.

    (A) fascinating . . defiant
    (B) anomalous . . fearful
    (C) splendid . . indifferent
    (D) disdainful . . perplexed
    (E) majestic . . awestruck

4. The accident resulted from ------- of unfortunate events; many factors came together to create the dangerous conditions.

    (A) a monopoly
    (B) a coincidence
    (C) a divergence
    (D) a repudiation
    (E) an elimination

5. Often ------- and -------, much of the country's workforce gets too little sleep and too little exercise.

    (A) cranky . . forlorn
    (B) vehement . . coercive
    (C) juvenile . . heedless
    (D) overextended . . flabby
    (E) exhilarated . . careful

6. Nguyen prided himself on his -------, an understanding of others' feelings that has earned him many friends.

   (A) empathy
   (B) temerity
   (C) astuteness
   (D) lethargy
   (E) sociability

7. The butcher, an especially ------- and devious man, often swindled his customers by rigging the scales in his shop.

   (A) furtive
   (B) bellicose
   (C) perceptive
   (D) emotive
   (E) diligent

8. Tonya's ------- in social situations became obvious when she offended the host by asking about his income at the party.

   (A) profligacy
   (B) mendacity
   (C) turpitude
   (D) gaucheness
   (E) severity

9. Though automobiles were relatively scarce in the first decades of the twentieth century, by 1950 they had ------- to the point of -------.

   (A) amalgamated . . invisibility
   (B) aggrandized . . ambivalence
   (C) proliferated . . ubiquity
   (D) evolved . . fruition
   (E) regressed . . dependability

ANSWERS & EXPLANATIONS

1. **E**

The main clause lets you know that the project *required more funding than the state could* -------. The blank here must mean something like "give." Your next move will be to scan the first word of each pair in the choices to see whether any match your prediction.

Demand, review, and *justify* don't mean "give." Eliminate **A**, **C**, and **D**. What about *renege* and *allocate*? If you know these words, you know that *renege* means "to go back on a promise" and *allocate* means "to distribute." **E** is a better choice. If you don't know these words, you can move on to the second blank. Since the state couldn't provide the money, *the highway commission proposed working in* ------- *private sources*. The second blank must mean something like "cooperation." Since you've already narrowed the choices down to **B** and **E**, you need to consider *in place of* and *in association with*. Which means "cooperation"? Only *in association with*.

Plug **E** into the sentence: *The highway construction project required more funding than the state could allocate, so the highway commission proposed working in association with private sources*. **E** is correct.

2. **C**

The opening modifier, *reacting to reviews that called his work childish and* -------, plays off the main clause, in which the artist wants *to convey maturity and* -------. Since the artist's reaction to being called *childish* was to try to *convey maturity*, which is opposite, the two blanks must have opposite meanings as well.

Now you need to scan the choices, looking for pairs with opposite meanings. *Irresponsible* and *sincerity*? Do those contrast? Not necessarily; eliminate **A**. *Meaningless* and *simplicity*? Not really; eliminate **B**. *Vulgar* and *refinement*? Something that's *vulgar* is tacky and something that has *refinement* is elegant. These are opposites; keep **C**. *Tedious* and *generosity*? Not opposites; nix **D**. *Obscure* and *decisiveness*? Not opposites; eliminate **E**. Read **C** back into the sentence: *Reacting to reviews that called his work childish and vulgar, the artist began his next series of paintings with a determination to convey maturity and refinement.* **C** is correct.

3. **E**

The first part of the sentence simply states that *Siberian tigers are considered among the most ------- of animals*. The second part, though, states that the tigers have *striking coloration, powerful musculature,* and *aloof bearing,* which *leave many people -------*. So the blanks will convey more or less the same idea: that the Siberian tiger is striking, powerful, and aloof. Which words in the first column could convey this idea? *Fascinating*? Possibly; keep **A**. *Anomalous*? Not really; eliminate **B**. *Splendid*? Possibly; keep **C**. *Disdainful*? No; eliminate **D**. *Majestic*? Possibly; keep **E**. Now, among **A**, **C**, and **E**, which is the best choice?

Take a look at the second word in each choice and keep in mind that you need something that continues the idea of the first word. Does *defiant* continue the idea of *fascinating*? No; eliminate **A**. Does *indifferent* continue the idea of *splendid*? No; eliminate **C**. Does *awestruck* continue the idea of *majestic*? Yes; keep **E**. Read **E** back into the sentence: *Siberian tigers are considered among the most majestic of animals; their striking coloration, powerful musculature, and aloof bearing leave many people awestruck.* **E** is correct.

4. **B**

The first part of the sentence tells you that the *accident resulted from a ------- of unfortunate events*. The second part tells you that *many factors came together to create the dangerous conditions*. So the blank must somehow convey the idea that the accident resulted from unfortunate events coming together to create dangerous conditions. You can predict that the blank will mean something like "happening at the same time."

Scanning the choices, which words could mean "happening at the same time"? *Monopoly* means "total control over the sale or production of a good or service"; eliminate **A**. *Coincidence* means "an occurrence of two or more events at the same time"; keep **B**. *Divergence* means "a departure from"; eliminate **C**. *Repudiation* means "rejection"; eliminate **D**. *Elimination* means "removal of"; get rid of **E**. Read **B** into the sentence: *The accident resulted from a coincidence of unfortunate events; many factors came together to create the dangerous conditions.*

5. **D**

The opening modifier, *often ------- and -------*, contains two blanks that correspond to *too little sleep and too little exercise* in the main clause. So you need a pair of words that convey those meanings. You can predict the first blank will mean "tired" and the second blank will mean "out of shape."

Scanning the choices for the first word, *cranky* and *overextended* have the desired meaning, while *vehement, juvenile,* and *exhilarated* do not. So keep **A** and **D**, and eliminate **B**, **C**, and **E**. The second words of **A** and **D** are *forlorn* and *flabby*, respectively. *Forlorn* doesn't match "out of shape," so eliminate **A**. *Flabby* does match "out of shape," so read **D** into the sentence: *Often overextended and flabby, much of the country's workforce gets too little sleep and too little exercise.* **D** is correct.

6. **A**

The sentence makes it clear that Nguyen prides himself on his *understanding of others' feelings*. You need to find a word that describes that type of understanding. You can predict you'll need a word like "compassion."

Scanning the choices, *empathy* means "understanding of another's feelings"; keep **A**. *Temerity* means "disregard of danger"; eliminate **B**. *Astuteness* means "keen judgment"; eliminate **C**. *Lethargy* means "lack of energy"; eliminate **D**. *Sociability* means "the quality of being friendly." This may seem tempting, but remember that you're not looking for "friendliness," but for "compassion." These aren't the same things; eliminate **E**. Plug **A** into the sentence: *Nguyen prided himself on his empathy, an understanding of others' feelings that has earned him many friends.* **A** is correct.

7. **A**

You know that the butcher is *especially ------- and devious* and that he *often swindled his customers*. So you need a word, like *devious* and *swindled*, that fits in with the idea of the butcher as "dishonest."

Scanning the choices, *furtive* means "secretive"; keep **A**. *Bellicose* means "warlike"; eliminate **B**. *Perceptive* means "insightful"; eliminate **C**. *Emotive* means "exhibiting emotion"; eliminate **D**. *Diligent* means "willing to put in effort"; eliminate **E**. Read **A** into the sentence: *The butcher, an especially furtive and devious man, often swindled his customers by rigging the scales in his shop.* **A** is correct.

8. **D**

Tonya doesn't seem to have very good social skills, given her awkward behavior at the party. You can predict that you're going to need a word that describes an inability to know how to conduct yourself in social situations. Something like "tactlessness."

Scanning the choices, *profligacy* means "wastefulness"; eliminate **A**. *Mendacity* means "untruthfulness"; eliminate **B**. *Turpitude* means "lack of morality"; eliminate **C**. *Gaucheness* means "tactlessness"; keep **D**. *Severity* means "harshness"; eliminate **E**. Read **D** into the sentence: *Tonya's gaucheness in social situations became obvious when she offended the host by asking about his income at the party.* **D** is correct.

9. **C**

When an item begins with *though*, chances are you're dealing with a contrast. In this item, the contrast is between the fact that autos were *relatively scarce in the first decades of the twentieth century* and the fact that *by 1950 they had ------- to the point of -------*. So you need two words that will convey the idea that cars became more common after 1950. The first blank is probably easier to handle and will probably mean something like "become more numerous."

Scanning the first words in the choices, *amalgamated* means "mixed," so eliminate **A**. *Aggrandized* means "made more important"; eliminate **B**. *Proliferated* means "increased in number"; keep **C**. *Evolved* means "developed gradually"; eliminate **D**. *Regressed* means "returned to a worse condition"; eliminate **E**. The second word in **C** is *ubiquity*, a tough word most people are not likely to know, but since only *proliferated* worked in the first blank, *ubiquity* must be correct for the second. Indeed it is. *Ubiquity* means "the state of being everywhere." That works in the context of this item. Read **C** into the sentence: *Though automobiles were relatively scarce in the first decades of the twentieth century, by 1950 they had proliferated to the point of ubiquity.* **C** is correct.

SENTENCE COMPLETIONS: PRACTICE SET 4

1. Vermeer's paintings were ------- by certain patrons during the artist's lifetime, but it was not until the nineteenth century, some three hundred years later, that he was universally -------.

    (A) collected . . praised
    (B) influenced . . rewarded
    (C) scorned . . promoted
    (D) relished . . dismissed
    (E) overseen . . guarded

2. Though the mayor claimed that he acted out of ------- when he ordered several new homeless shelters to be built, his critics maintained a more ------- view, insisting that the plans were actually to benefit a local contractor.

    (A) curiosity . . inaccurate
    (B) respect . . egalitarian
    (C) charity . . skeptical
    (D) frustration . . productive
    (E) determination . . complicated

3. Dante's *Divine Comedy*, written in three parts, is a ------- work that many people, daunted by the task of reading it in its entirety, often read it in its ------- form.

    (A) subtle . . universal
    (B) voluminous . . abridged
    (C) barbaric . . censored
    (D) morose . . unedited
    (E) tedious . . original

4. The dance program at the festival was -------, incorporating pieces from many different cultures and eras.

    (A) sporadic
    (B) impeccable
    (C) perilous
    (D) eclectic
    (E) lyrical

5. Candidates for public office often ------- popular views expressly to ------- public approval, even though the candidates do not necessarily hold those views personally.

    (A) deter . . aggravate
    (B) denounce . . replace
    (C) sanctify . . arouse
    (D) neglect . . impeach
    (E) espouse . . garner

6. Humans have a tendency to assign personality traits to whole species of animals, saying, for example, that cats are ------- because they like to explore and that dogs are ------- because they enjoy the company of people.

    (A) inspiring . . reverential
    (B) inquisitive . . gregarious
    (C) uninhibited . . dour
    (D) jovial . . despotic
    (E) reticent . . nurturing

7. Despite her general -------, Gretchen could often be ------- with people when she felt stressed.

    (A) affability . . brusque
    (B) reliability . . imprecise
    (C) contentment . . relentless
    (D) tenderness . . erratic
    (E) animosity . . obtuse

8. Recipes for watercolor paint caution against adding too much pigment, lest the paint become -------, resulting in watercolors that are too thick and sticky to work with properly.

    (A) translucent
    (B) ponderous
    (C) malleable
    (D) glutinous
    (E) vitiated

9. The ancient Romans valued ------- greatly; they considered the ability to speak ------- a true gift.

    (A) kinetics . . speciously
    (B) egotism . . spontaneously
    (C) rhetoric . . compellingly
    (D) dialogue . . imperiously
    (E) poetics . . sincerely

10. An avid fan of mystery novels, Warren loved to solve the crimes and asked his sister not to spoil the mystery book she had just read by revealing details of its -------.

    (A) aphorism
    (B) epitaph
    (C) preface
    (D) denouement
    (E) metaphor

ANSWERS & EXPLANATIONS

1. **A**

The main clause lets you know that *Vermeer's paintings were ------- by certain patrons during the artist's lifetime.* This is contrasted with the fact that *it was not until the nineteenth century, some three hundred years later, that he was universally -------*, which lets you know that the relationship between Vermeer and his patrons eventually expanded *universally.* What kind of relationship did Vermeer have with his patrons, though? A patron is someone who supports an artist, so you can predict that the first blank will mean something like "supported."

Scanning the choices, *collected* in **A** could work with "supported," so keep **A**. *Influenced* doesn't match; eliminate **B**. *Scorned* is the opposite of what you need; eliminate **C**. *Relished* could possibly work; hang on to **D**. *Overseen* doesn't really make sense with *supported*; eliminate **E**. Now you're down to **A** and **D**. The second word in **A** is *praised*, which makes sense in the context of the sentence; keep **A**. The second word in **D** is *dismissed*, which doesn't work.

Get rid of **D**. Plug **A** into the sentence: *Vermeer's paintings were collected by certain patrons during the artist's lifetime, but it was not until the nineteenth century, some three hundred years later, that he was universally praised.* **A** is correct.

2.   **C**

You know the mayor built some homeless shelters, claiming that *he acted out of* ------- in doing so, but that his critics, who are likely to mistrust the mayor, thought *the plans were actually to benefit a local contractor.* So you know that the critics doubted the mayor's given reason for building the shelters. The second blank is probably easier to handle here, since you need to show that the critics doubted the mayor. You can predict that the second word will mean "doubting."

Scanning the second words of the choices, only *skeptical* in **C** conveys the meaning of "doubting." The first word in **C**, *charity*, also works in this context, since the mayor was building homeless shelters, which he could easily claim as an act of charity. Plug **C** into the sentence: *Though the mayor claimed that he acted out of charity when he ordered several new homeless shelters to be built, his critics maintained a more skeptical view, insisting that the plans were actually to benefit a local contractor.* **C** is correct.

3.   **B**

The first blank describes the book, which you know was *written in three parts*. The sentence then goes on to explain that *many people* are *daunted by the task of reading it in its entirety*. So the first blank should convey the sense of "long."

Scanning the choices, only *voluminous* in **B** and *tedious* in **E** have meanings compatible with "long." Keep them; eliminate **A**, **C**, and **D**. Now, for the second blank, the sentence lets you know that, because people are *daunted by the task of reading* the book *in its entirety*, they *often read* it *in its* ------- *form*. If they don't want to read the whole book, they probably read it in a shortened version. So the second blank should mean something like "shortened."

If you look at the second words of **B** and **E**, *abridged* and *original*, respectively, only *abridged* has the desired meaning. Plug **B** into the sentence: *Dante's Divine Comedy, written in three parts, is a voluminous work that many people, daunted by the task of reading it in its entirety, often read it in its abridged form.* **B** is correct.

4.   **D**

The main clause contains the blank describing the *dance program*. The modifier, though, tells you that it incorporates *pieces from many different cultures and eras*. So the blank must convey the meaning of *incorporating pieces from many different cultures and eras*. You can predict that you'll need a word that means "diverse."

Scanning the choices, *sporadic* means "happening now and then"; eliminate **A**. *Impeccable* means "unblemished"; eliminate **B**. *Perilous* means "dangerous"; eliminate **C**. *Eclectic* means "diverse"; keep **D**. *Lyrical* means "poetic"; eliminate **E**. Plug **D** into the sentence: *The dance program at the festival was eclectic, incorporating pieces from many different cultures and eras.* **D** is correct.

5.   **E**

The main clause tells you that *candidates for public office often* ------- *popular views expressly to* ------- *public approval*. You know from the last clause of the sentence that *the candidates do not necessarily hold those views personally*. So the candidates use those views to gain approval to win votes. So the first blank must mean something like "adopt" and the second "gain."

Scanning the choices, *deter*, *denounce*, and *neglect* don't mean "adopt," so eliminate **A**, **B**, and **D**. *Sanctify* and *espouse* might be harder to define, so keep them. Look at the second words in **C** and **E**. In **C**, you have *arouse*. Does that make sense in this context? Not really. What about *garner* in **E**? To *garner* means "to earn," which is compatible with "gain," your prediction. Keep **E** and plug it into the sentence: *Candidates for public office often espouse popular views expressly to garner public approval, even though the candidates do not necessarily hold those views personally.* **E** is correct.

6. **B**

The relative clause states *that cats are ------- because they like to explore and that dogs are ------- because they enjoy the company of people.* So you know you need for the first blank a word that means "likes to explore" and for the second a word that means "enjoys the company of people."

Scanning the choices for the first word, *inquisitive* in **B** and *uninhibited* in **C** are possibilities, Eliminate **A**, **D**, and **E**. Which is closer to "enjoys the company of people," *gregarious* in **B** or *dour* in **C**? Since *dour* means "glum and unpleasant," it's probably not the best choice. Eliminate **C**. Read **B** into the sentence: *Humans have a tendency to assign personality traits to whole species of animals, saying, for example, that cats are inquisitive because they like to explore and that dogs are gregarious because they enjoy the company of people.* **B** is correct.

7. **A**

Despite tells you right off the bat that you're dealing with a contrast item. So *despite her general ------, Gretchen could often be -------.* The two blanks will be contradictory. The word in the second blank applies to Gretchen when she feels stressed, so it's probably a negative word, something meaning "not friendly or nice." You can begin looking for the second word first.

Scanning the second words in the choices, *brusque* means "gruff." That fits your prediction, so keep **A**. *Imprecise* means "not specific"; eliminate **B**. *Relentless* means "unwilling to give up"; eliminate **C**. *Erratic* means "unpredictable"; eliminate **D**. *Obtuse* means "thickheaded"; get rid of **E**. Check the first word of **A**: *affability*. It means "friendliness." That stands in contrast to *brusque*, so **A** still looks like a winner. Plug it into the sentence: *Despite her general affability, Gretchen could often be brusque with people when she felt stressed.* **A** is correct.

8. **D**

The recipes *caution against adding too much pigment, lest the paint become -------.* Become what? *Too thick and sticky to work with properly.* So you need a work that means "thick and sticky."

Scanning the choices, *translucent* means "allowing light to pass through"; eliminate **A**. *Ponderous* means "weighty and serious"; eliminate **B**. *Malleable* means "able to be shaped and molded"; eliminate **C**. *Glutinous* means "thick and sticky"; keep **D**. *Vitiated* means "made impure"; eliminate **E**. Plug **D** into the sentence: *Recipes for watercolor paint caution against adding too much pigment, lest the paint become glutinous, resulting in watercolors that are too thick and sticky to work with properly.* **D** is correct.

9. **C**

The first part of the sentence tells you that *the ancient Romans valued ------- greatly.* The second part tells you that *they considered the ability to speak ------- a true gift.* So you know that the first blank must have something to do with "speaking" and the second with speaking "well."

Scanning the first words of the choices, *kinetics* is "the science of motion"; eliminate **A**. *Egotism* is "selfishness"; eliminate **B**. *Rhetoric* is "persuasive speech or writing"; keep **C**. *Dialogue* is "a verbal exchange between two people"; keep **D**. *Poetics* is "the study of poetry"; perhaps vaguely related, but not close enough. Eliminate **E**. The second word in **C** is *compellingly*, which means "persuasively"; keep **C**. The second word in **D** is *imperiously*, which means "overbearing"; eliminate **D**. Plug **C** into the sentence: *The ancient Romans valued rhetoric greatly; they considered the ability to speak compellingly a true gift.* **C** is correct.

10. **D**

Warren loves to figure out whodunits and didn't want his sister to ruin the ending of the book for him. So you know the blank must mean "ending." Scanning the choices, *aphorism* means "witty saying"; eliminate **A**. *Epitaph* means "engraving on a tombstone"; eliminate **B**. *Preface* means "introductory statement in a book"; eliminate **C**. *Denouement* means "final outcome of the plot of a story"; keep **D**. *Metaphor* means "symbolism"; eliminate **E**. Plug **D** into the sentence: *An avid fan of mystery novels, Warren loved to solve the crimes and asked his sister not to spoil the mystery book she had just read by revealing details of its denouement.* **D** is correct.

the new SAT Critical Reading Workbook

SENTENCE COMPLETIONS: PRACTICE SET 5

1. The boss gave Marcie the promotion because of her ----; she always gets the job done quickly.

    (A) expedience
    (B) laboriousness
    (C) reticence
    (D) frugality
    (E) pathos

2. During his speech, Alex continuously wiped sweat off of his brow, signaling his ----.

    (A) ambivalence
    (B) brashness
    (C) tactfulness
    (D) agitation
    (E) tranquility

3. Aspirin has recently been lauded as a ----; many experts believe that it can ---- all sorts of illnesses.

    (A) blight...exacerbate
    (B) plague...exaggerate
    (C) panacea...alleviate
    (D) paregoric...induce
    (E) pandemic...incite

4. Drinking one alcoholic drink per day is strongly ---- by many doctors for its health benefits.

    (A) advocated
    (B) dictated
    (C) forbidden
    (D) disallowed
    (E) banned

5. Rita was obviously ---- about her last boyfriend's behavior; she shredded his picture into tiny pieces and muttered under her breath after their breakup.

    (A) incensed
    (B) apprehensive
    (C) apathetic
    (D) ignorant
    (E) sentimental

6. The ballet teacher ---- her students often; she would not accept ---- effort.

    (A) pampered...strenuous
    (B) placated...arduous
    (C) patronized...minimal
    (D) lambasted...trivial
    (E) persecuted...minute

7.   Many people were ---- when the quiet, prudent science teacher suddenly eloped.

(A) flabbergasted
(B) petulant
(C) affable
(D) indifferent
(E) disinterested

8.   Sheri has always been ----; her last high test score ---- her brilliance.

(A) inane...belied
(B) astute...underscored
(C) ostentatious...disproved
(D) ingenious...miscast
(E) boorish...reiterated

9.   Running is a ---- sport; as a result, runners often experience ---- effects of running, such as shin splints, twisted ankles, and knee problems.

(A) lackadaisical...euphoric
(B) rigorous...deleterious
(C) arduous...admirable
(D) leisure...unfortunate
(E) taxing...gratifying

10. Because Miss Jones never married and has five cats, many take her for a(n) ---- old maid.

(A) fastidious
(B) atypical
(C) obstreperous
(D) bellicose
(E) obtuse

ANSWERS AND EXPLANATIONS

1.   **A**

The clue word "quickly," suggests that the missing word is a synonym of this word. So, *laboriousness* would not work since it implies slow labor, and neither would *reticence*, since it means "slow to do something". Likewise, *frugality* has nothing to do with speed, and *pathos*, or sympathy, does not either. So, the correct answer is **A**, expedience.

2.   **D**

Because wiping sweat off of one's brow usually signals nervousness, the word that fits in the blank should be one with a similar meaning. Thus, *ambivalence* can be eliminated since it means "confusion about an issue". Likewise, *brashness* may be deleted as a possibility since it implies boldness. *Tactfulness* and *tranquility* may also be eliminated as choices since the speaker is neither mannerly or at peace. The correct answer is then **D**, *agitation*.

3.   **C**

Because of the clue word "lauded," one can expect the blanks to be filled with positive words. Thus, choices **A**, **B**, and **E** may all be eliminated since they refer to worldwide diseases. Choice **D** may also be eliminated since *paregoric* refers to an opium tincture. Thus, the correct answer is **C**, *panacea*, meaning "remedy or cure-all".

4.   **A**

Because having one drink a day has health benefits, it may be assumed that doctors want patients to consume one drink per day. Thus, answers **C**, **D**, and **E** may be eliminated. Answer

B seems like a good choice, but most doctors would not have *dictated* that a patient do anything. Thus, **A**, *advocated*, meaning "suggested", is the best answer.

5.   **A**

Since Rita's behavior suggests anger, a synonym of that emotion would likely fit in the blank. Thus, **B**, **C**, **D**, and **E** can quickly be eliminated since they do not suggest anger. The correct choice is **A**, *incensed*.

6.   **D**

The ballet teacher obviously pushes her students to do their best. Thus, the first words, *pampered*, *placated*, and *patronized* must rule out **A**, **B**, and **C** as possible answers. Answer **E** can be ruled out because it is too harsh. A good teacher would never have *persecuted* her students. Thus, **D**, *lambasted...trivial*, meaning "to assault verbally...unimportant", is the correct answer.

7.   **A**

Because her actions are surprising, the answer should reflect people's stunned reaction. Thus, **D** and **E** may be immediately ruled out since these words mean "not surprised". Also, **B** may be eliminated since a *petulant*, or angry, reaction would not fit the situation. **C** may be done away with, as well, since the people were not necessarily *affable*, or agreeable, to such an occurence. Thus, **A**, *flabbergasted*, is the correct answer.

8.   **B**

Since the sentence states that Sheri is brilliant, the first blank should have a word that means the same as the word "brilliant." **A**, *inane*, meaning "stupid", **C**, *ostentatious*, meaning "pretentious", and **E**, *boorish*, meaning "rude", can all be eliminated because none of these mean "brilliant." Answer **D** can be deleted as an option because of the word *miscast*. Thus, the correct answer is **B**, *astute* (clever) ...*underscored*.

9.   **B**

The construction of this sentence implies a relationship between the type of sport that running is and the physical effects it wreaks on the body. Thus, **A**, **D**, and **E** may be eliminated since running and its effects are not properly paired. Answer **C** will not work, because injuries such as those listed are not *admirable*. Thus, the answer is **B**, *rigorous* (demanding)..*deleterious* (harmful).

10.   **A**

Because Miss Jones is described as a stereotypical old maid, it seems that a typical descriptor would fit in the blank. So, **B**, **C**, *obstreperous*, meaning "noisy", **D**, *bellicose*, meaning "warlike", and **E**, *obtuse*, meaning "dense or dull", can all be eliminated since they would not be logical answers. The correct answer is **A**, *fastidious*, meaning "particular" or "given to routine".

SENTENCE COMPLETIONS: PRACTICE SET 6

1. Although the students liked the new professor, they found his class to be ---- because of its weekly tests, quizzes, and lengthy papers.

   (A) facile
   (B) pedantic
   (C) bovine
   (D) arduous
   (E) animated

2. Because of his bad behavior toward women, attendance at wild parties, and excessive drinking, Chris was known as a ----.

   (A) rapscallion
   (B) clergyman
   (C) knight
   (D) dandy
   (E) youngster

3. At first, the stylish, trendy store was a(n) ---- success, serving hundreds of customers each day; however, after its prices soared, it lost its appeal.

   (A) marginal
   (B) moderate
   (C) modest
   (D) immense
   (E) reasonable

4. Margie kept hearing ---- noises in her house; however, she thought she was ---- until a rat scampered across the floor one evening.

   (A) commonplace…deluded
   (B) extraordinary…foolhardy
   (C) daunting…cognizant
   (D) astounding…intuitive
   (E) foreign…discerning

5. John could tell from the look of ---- on Bonnie's face that she was not happy to see him.

   (A) consternation
   (B) nonchalance
   (C) ignorance
   (D) felicity
   (E) incredulity

the new SAT Critical Reading Workbook

6. A job in which one is paid solely on commissions can often be ----, since income is never guaranteed.

    (A) tenuous
    (B) consoling
    (C) opportune
    (D) rigid
    (E) astounding

7. Because of her downcast eyes and shy smile, Nancy is viewed as ---- by most people.

    (A) lugubrious
    (B) demure
    (C) ingenious
    (D) raucous
    (E) derisive

8. The seasoned employees did not appreciate the young man's ---- attitude.

    (A) compliant
    (B) unpretentious
    (C) amicable
    (D) perfidious
    (E) reputable

9. Lara could not get used to the ---- northern weather; the snow never seemed to ----.

    (A) blustery...dissipate
    (B) temperate...commence
    (C) balmy...evaporate
    (D) moderate...cease
    (E) tempestuous...accrue

10. Although the speaker had ---- ideas, he could not seem to organize them and was described by many listeners as ----.

    (A) intriguing...discombobulated
    (B) vapid...eloquent
    (C) pedantic...loquacious
    (D) base...glib
    (E) spirited...voluble

ANSWERS & EXPLANATIONS

1. **D**

The major clue in this sentence is the list of the assignments and tasks that the class requires. Since there are so many requirements, one might assume that the class is difficult. Thus, the most logical answer would be **D**, *arduous*. Unfamiliar vocabulary may include these words: *facile* (easy), *pedantic* (showing off one's knowledge), and *bovine* (cow-like).

2. **A**

Because of his bad behavior, one would expect the answer to be descriptive of a man with such behavior. Thus, *knight, youngster*, and *clergyman* can be immediately eliminated. *Dandy* might seem to be a good answer, but it is more descriptive of a man who is very concerned with dress and social appearances. So, *rapscallion*, **A**, is the best answer.

3. **D**

Because this store serviced hundreds of customers when it first opened, one might assume that it experienced more than a *marginal, moderate, reasonable,* or *modest* success. It was an *immense* success, **D**.

4. **B**

Answer **A** may be eliminated since the sounds are apparently not *commonplace*, or everyday sounds. **C, D,** and **E** may be removed as choices, too, because the second word in each pair does not describe the woman's skepticism of what she hears. However, **B** does. Thus, the answer is *extraordinary…foolhardy.*

5. **A**

Since Bonnie does not look happy to see John, the word that fits in the blank has something to do with sadness or anger. Thus, *felicity,* or happiness, can be ruled out, as can *nonchalance,* or indifference. *Ignorance* can also be eliminated since someone showing ignorance would probably be neither happy nor sad. Also, *incredulity* may be removed since it simply means that something is "not believable" and "only intimates surprise". So, the correct answer is **A**, *consternation,* meaning "anger".

6. **A**

It stands to reason that a job worked solely on commission would be uncertain. Thus, the word that fits in the blank is most likely a synonym of the word "uncertain." *Consoling* and *opportune* can quickly be eliminated, as they are positive words, and such a job would certainly have its ups and downs. *Astounding* does not make sense in the sentence and can be removed as an option. Likewise, a job based on commission would not be *rigid,* or predictable, so that choice may be eliminated. Clearly, the answer is **A**, *tenuous,* meaning "uncertain."

7. **B**

Because of her mannerisms, Nancy might be described as shy. So, *raucous,* meaning "loud and noisy", can be ruled out as an answer. Also, *lugubrious,* meaning "mournful", can be eliminated. Likewise, *ingenious* and *derisive* may be removed as options because they do not logically link with shyness. So, the correct answer is **B**, *demure,* or shy.

8. **D**

A, B, C, and **E** may be ruled out as answers since seasoned employees would have no problem with a person described in friendly and respectable terms. The correct answer, then, is **D**, *perfidious,* meaning "dishonest."

9. **A**

B, C, and **D** may be ruled out since these adjectives do not usually describe snowy, cold conditions. *Tempestuous* is tempting, but its partnered word, *accrue,* does not make sense. So, the answer is **A**.

10. **A**

B, *vapid,* meaning "boring", **C**, *pedantic,* or showing off one's knowledge, and **D**, *base,* which means "of the lowest level", may be ruled out as answers since the speaker obviously has interesting content and the first words of each of these pairs contradicts that notion. **E** does not work because of the last word, *voluble,* meaning "talkative." Disorganized and talkative are not synonyms; thus, answer **A** is correct.

SENTENCE COMPLETIONS: PRACTICE SET 7

SENTENCE COMPLETIONS: PRACTICE SET 7

1. Scientists have recently stated that *acrylimide*, a chemical found in some fried foods, may be ----- to the development of fetuses, causing cancer later in life.

   (A) detrimental
   (B) salutary
   (C) amicable
   (D) advantageous
   (E) salubrious

2. Ryan has one very --- habit: he always picks his nose in public.

   (A) hale
   (B) robust
   (C) noxious
   (D) cultivated
   (E) refined

3. Nat King Cole was a(n) ---- jazz singer whose voice still echoes on radio today; interestingly, he always ---- the many cigarettes he smoked each day as his secret.

   (A) mediocre...hailed
   (B) phenomenal...credited
   (C) incompetent...praised
   (D) groveling...lauded
   (E) liminal...extolled

4. Stress during pregnancy ---- the risk of early delivery; such women may deliver on or before 37 weeks of pregnancy.

   (A) modifies
   (B) exacerbates
   (C) decimates
   (D) alleviates
   (E) denigrates

5. Lucy often blames her lack of friends on her ----, although she is not extremely overweight.

   (A) comeliness
   (B) gauntness
   (C) corpulence
   (D) svelteness
   (E) fecundity

6.   Joe is a(n) ---- actor who always keeps his audiences entertained; however, he only lands ----
     roles that do not pay his bills.

   (A) brilliant...acclaimed
   (B) inane...scant
   (C) inept...grandiose
   (D) adroit...paltry
   (E) apt...glamorous

7.   Sally has a(n) ---- nature; she seems to float in and out of rooms without people noticing her.

   (A) ephemeral
   (B) stolid
   (C) garrulous
   (D) ghastly
   (E) obsequious

8.   Lorna always thought that raising children would be ---- since her own mother raised six
     children with seemingly no effort; however, she told me that it is the most ---- task she has
     ever performed.

   (A) facile...minute
   (B) uncomplicated...severe
   (C) leisurely...eccentric
   (D) laborious...perplexing
   (E) harrowing...ghastly

9.   Alan always chooses the most ---- Halloween costume each year; last year he was Dracula, and
     he frightened everyone out of their wits with his fangs, fake blood and generally ----
     appearance.

   (A) benign..comely
   (B) ghastly..gory
   (C) ostentatious..radiant
   (D) macabre..celestial
   (E) titillating..naive

10. Mark realized too late that Anna's intentions were ----; she tricked him before he knew what
     had happened.

   (A) benevolent
   (B) virtuous
   (C) perfidious
   (D) insolent
   (E) mundane

ANSWERS & EXPLANATIONS

1.   **A**

B, **C**, **D**, and **E** may be eliminated since all of them suggest that this chemical is harmless or
even healthy for fetuses. Thus, **A**, *detrimental*, meaning "harmful", is the correct answer.

2.   **C**

A and **B** may be eliminated since both of these words mean "healthy", and this habit certainly
is not a healthy one. **D** and **E** may also be removed as options since both of these choices mean
"mannerly." So, answer **C**, *noxious*, meaning "disgusting", is the correct answer.

3. **B**

Because Cole's songs are still played on the radio today, one may assume that he was a very popular singer. Thus, all of the pairs may be eliminated, except for **B**, since they make light of his talent or cast him as a mediocre singer. So, the correct answer is **B**. Unfamiliar vocabulary may include these words: **D**, *groveling*, which means "crawling", and **E**, *liminal*, which pertains to threshold.

4. **B**

A may be ruled out because of the evidence in the sentence that suggests that stress increases the possibility of premature labor. **C**, **D**, and **E** may also be eliminated because all of these words mean that stress reduces the likelihood of premature labor. Thus, **B**, *exacerbates*, meaning "to make worse", is the correct answer.

5. **C**

Since that the sentence suggests that Lucy is large, or at least thinks she is overweight, the word that fits in the blank must be a synonym for obesity. Thus, **C** is the correct answer.

6. **D**

B and **C** may be eliminated because context clues indicate that Joe is a good actor. **A** and **E** may also be removed, because they do not fit exactly into the context of the last blank. The word needed concerns a low-paying job. Thus, **D**, *adroit*, meaning "clever", is the correct answer.

7. **A**

The clues in this sentence are that Sally seems to "float" and that no one notices her. Thus, her presence is fleeting, and she is **A**, *ephemeral*.

8. **B**

Since Lorna relies on her mother's own experience in raising children, she expects her own childrearing to be the same way. Thus, the first blank must be filled with a word meaning "easy." So, **D** and **E** may be omitted as answers. **B** is the best answer, because Lorna finds the task to be **B**, *severe*, rather than *uncomplicated*.

9. **B**

A, **C**, and **E** may be eliminated because one of the two words does not fit the idea of Halloween and Dracula. **D** looks good, at first, because of the word *macabre*, meaning "gory", but the word *celestial*, meaning "heavenly", does not work. So, the correct answer is **B**.

10. **C**

A, **B**, and **E** are not compatible with out contextual clue, "tricked." Insolent might be a consideration, but it does not fit with a person who likes to deceive others. Thus, the correct answer is **C**, *perfidious*, which means "faithless."

reading
passages

TO MAKE A LONG STORY SHORT, THE SAT NOW CONTAINS two kinds of critical reading passages (which we call RPs):

- The familiar long RPs—multiparagraph passages followed by a series of questions.
- New short RPs—brief one-paragraph passages followed by two questions.

The test also contains dual passages for both long and short RPs that require you to read two passages and answer questions about how they relate. Long and short RP questions account for about two-thirds of the entire SAT Critical Reading section. Explaining what they're all about and how to beat them accounts for 100 percent of the next three chapters.

BECOME A READING MACHINE

Whether you're dealing with long or short reading passages, you've got to have critical reading skills. But you can't just study for reading passages as easily as you can for math or grammar. If you don't know how to deal with triangles, you can study the precise rules that apply to *all* triangles. But if you're having trouble getting through reading passages, it's not quite as easy to figure out what to do.

So how *do* you study for reading passages? The answer is simple: Thou shalt read. Read! Read like mad. From this instant until the day you take the SAT, read, read, read. Reeeeeead. But don't read like you watch TV. You need to keep your mind *active* as you read, look between the lines and think about the mechanics, or the inner workings, of everything you read. For example,

1. **What's the author's main point or purpose?** Does the author, for instance, argue that lyrics to pop songs will corrupt America's youth?
2. **How does the author's attitude relate to the point being made?** Does the writer talk about pop stars in tones of disgust or of admiration?
3. **How does the author use language, sentence structure, and rhetorical devices, such as similes and metaphors?** Perhaps the writer is shocked by a pop star's new look and compares her to a siren, a character from Greek mythology who lured men to their dooms.

The point here is to train yourself to keep your brain on SAT alert while you read. Don't just coast. If you ask questions about what's going on as you read in your daily life, when the new SAT comes along, the RP questions will just feel like extensions of the reading mastery you've already established.

SLAYING THE FIRE-BREATHING JARGON

The new SAT includes questions about rhetorical devices on both long and short RPs. Rhetorical devices are tools that authors use to convey meaning or add depth and richness to their writing. Terms such as *simile*, *metaphor*, and *personification* are rhetorical devices. Jargon's in, so now you've got to figure jargon out.

If you think this decision confirms that the new SAT overhaul is really more like The SAT Gone Wild, we don't necessarily disagree. But consider this: You'll have to recognize and analyze rhetorical devices in literature throughout high school and college. Learning these terms now will actually prove useful to your education beyond studying for the SAT. To help you get the most important rhetorical devices down cold, here's a list of the top 25 terms that will most likely appear on the new SAT:

- **Alliteration**—The repetition of similar sounds, usually consonants, at the beginning of words. "Sweet scented stuff" is an example of alliteration in Robert Frost's poem "Out, Out—."

- **Allusion**—A reference within a literary work to a historical, literary, or biblical character, place, or event. The following line from Shakespeare's *The Merchant of Venice* contains an allusion to the Roman mythological character Cupid: "Come, come, Nerissa; for I long to see quick Cupid's post that comes so mannerly."

- **Assonance**—The repetition of vowel sounds in a sequence of nearby words. "The monster spoke in a low mellow tone" has assonance in its repetition of the "o" sound.

- **Caricature**—A description or characterization that exaggerates or distorts a character's prominent features, usually for purposes of mockery. A cartoon of Abraham Lincoln with a giant top hat, a very thick beard, and extremely sunken eyes could be considered a caricature.

- **Cliché**—A familiar expression that has been used and reused so many times that it's lost its expressive power. "Happy as a clam" or "eyes like a hawk" are examples of clichés.

- **Epiphany**—A sudden, powerful, and often spiritual or life-changing realization that a character experiences in an otherwise ordinary moment.

- **Foreshadowing**—An author's deliberate use of hints or suggestions to give a preview of events or themes that do not develop until later in the narrative. Images such as a storm brewing or a crow landing on a fencepost often foreshadow ominous developments in a story.

- **Hyperbole**—An excessive overstatement or exaggeration of fact. "I've told you that a million times already" is a hyperbolic statement.

- **Idiom**—A common expression that has acquired a meaning that differs from its literal meaning, such as "It's raining cats and dogs" or "That cost me an arm and a leg."

- **Imagery**—Language that brings to mind sensory impressions. Homer's description of dawn as "rosy-fingered" in the *Odyssey* is an example of his use of imagery.

- **Irony**—**Irony** usually emphasizes the contrast between the way things are expected to be and the way they actually are. Here's an example of irony: Medieval people believed that bathing would harm them when in fact *not* bathing led to the unsanitary conditions that caused the bubonic plague.

- **Metaphor**—The comparison of one thing to another that does not use the terms *like* or *as*. Metaphors use a form of the verb "to be" to establish a comparison. A metaphor from Shakespeare's *Macbeth*: "Life is but a walking shadow."

- **Motif**—A recurring structure, contrast, idea, or other device that develops a literary work's major ideas. Urban decay is a motif in the novel *1984*, which is filled with scenes of a dilapidated, rundown city. Shadows and darkness is a motif in *A Tale of Two Cities*, a novel that contains many dreary, gloomy scenes and settings.

- **Onomatopoeia**—The use of words such as *pop* or *hiss* where the spoken sound resembles the actual sound. "The *whoosh* of the waves at the seashore," and "The *zoom* of the race cars speeding around the track" are two examples of **onomatopoeia**.

- **Oxymoron**—The association of two terms that seem to contradict each other, as in the expression "wise fool" or "jumbo shrimp."

- **Paradox**—A statement that seems contradictory on the surface but often expresses a deeper truth. The line from Oscar Wilde's *The Ballad of Reading Gaol*, "All men destroy the things they love" is a paradox.

- **Personification**—The use of human characteristics to describe animals, things, or ideas. Using the word "babbling" to describe a brook is an example of **personification**.
- **Pun**—A play on words that uses the similarity in sound between two words with distinctly different meanings. For example, the title of Oscar Wilde's play *The Importance of Being Earnest* is a pun on the word *earnest*, which means "serious" or "sober," and the name "Ernest."
- **Rhetorical Question**—A question asked not to elicit an actual response but to make an impact or call attention to something. "Will the world ever see the end of war?" is an example of a rhetorical question.
- **Sarcasm**—A verbal tone in which it is obvious from context that the speaker means the opposite of what he or she says. "Mom, I'd love to see *Howard the Duck* with you" is probably a phrase you would say sarcastically.
- **Simile**—A comparison of two things that uses the words *like* or *as*. "Love is like a fire" is a simile.
- **Symbol**—An object, character, figure, place, or color used to represent an abstract idea or concept. The two roads in Robert Frost's poem "The Road Not Taken" **symbolize** the choice between two paths in life.
- **Theme**—A fundamental and universal idea explored in a literary work. The struggle to achieve the American Dream is a common theme in twentieth-century American literature.
- **Thesis**—The central argument that an author tries to make in a literary work. Some might consider J. D. Salinger's thesis in *The Catcher in the Rye* that society often forces people to be phoney.
- **Tone**—The author's or narrator's attitude toward the story or the subject. The tone of the *Declaration of Independence* is determined and confident.

RP SIZE AND RP SKILL

The difference between short RP questions and long RP questions is not in the questions. The questions are actually quite similar. The difference—prepare to be shocked—is in the *length* of the passages. Short RPs are about 100-words long and are followed by two questions. Long RPs are 500 to 800 words and include anywhere from eight to thirteen questions.

So, the questions on long and short RPs are similar, but the passages are of vastly different lengths. What should this mean to you? Two things:

1. **Long and short RPs test the same skills:** Your ability to understand what an author is trying to say and your ability to evaluate how an author uses language to make his or her points.
2. **Your strategy for dealing with long and short RPs has to be different.** The vast difference in the length of the passages affects how you should think about reading the passage and how you should deal with the questions after the passage.

In the following two chapters, we teach you the strategies you need to meet and beat both long and short RPs.

THE LONG OF IT

LONG READING PASSAGES POSE A DOUBLE CHALLENGE: Just like on every other section of the new SAT, you have to know how to deal with each individual question. But you also need a strategy for dealing with the passage. In this chapter, we show you how to deal with all the different types of questions the Critical Reading section might throw at you, *and* we explain the best strategy for how to read and remember the passage.

INSTRUCTIONS FOR READING PASSAGES

Here's your first RP exercise:

> Each passage below is followed by questions based on its content. Answer the questions following each passage on the basis of what is stated or implied in that passage and in any introductory material that may be provided.

WHAT THE INSTRUCTIONS DON'T TELL YOU

The instructions gloss over two important facts about reading passages and questions. Here they are:

- **Don't skip over the italicized contextual blurb**. Above each passage, you'll see an italicized introductory blurb that may offer some contextual information. The introduction looks a lot like instructions, and you know you're usually supposed to not waste time reading instructions that you can memorize long before taking the test. However, the context that the introduction provides will often help you understand the passage. So, read this introduction. Do not skip over it.
- **The order of the questions**. The questions following the passage are *not* ordered by difficulty. That means you should *not* adjust your pacing strategy on reading passages based on where a particular question appears relative to the other questions. The last few questions won't necessarily be tougher than the first few. Instead, RP questions are ordered by what part of the passage they refer to. Questions that test the beginning of the passage appear at the beginning of the group, questions that test the middle appear in the middle, and questions that cover the end appear at the end. General questions that cover the entire passage can appear either at the beginning or the end of the group of questions. General questions won't appear in the middle of the group.

A SAMPLE PASSAGE AND QUESTIONS

It's tough to talk about long RPs and questions without a sample passage and questions to look at. So, here's a sample passage about Galileo with the italicized introduction.

As you read the passage, note the little numbers to the left. Those numbers count off every five lines of the passage (the "5" means that you're reading the fifth line of the passage, the "10" means that you're reading the tenth line of the passage, and so on). Questions that ask you to refer to a specific word or section of the passage will include the line numbers of that word or section.

Sample Passage

The following passage discusses the scientific life of Galileo Galilei in reference to the political, religious, artistic, and scientific movements of the age.

Line

Galileo Galilei was born in 1564 into a Europe wracked by cultural ferment and religious strife. The popes of the Roman Catholic Church, powerful in their roles as both religious and secular leaders, had proven vulnerable to the worldly and decadent spirit of the age, and their personal immorality brought the reputation of the papacy to historic lows. In 1517, Martin

5 Luther, a former monk, attacked Catholicism for having become too worldly and politically corrupt and for obscuring the fundamentals of Christianity with pagan elements. His reforming zeal, which appealed to a notion of an original, "purified" Christianity, set in motion the Protestant Reformation and split European Christianity in two.

In response, Roman Catholicism steeled itself for battle and launched the Counter-Reformation, which emphasized orthodoxy and fidelity to the true Church. The Counter-
10 Reformation reinvigorated the Church and, to some extent, eliminated its excesses. But the Counter-Reformation also contributed to the decline of the Italian Renaissance, a revival of arts and letters that sought to recover and rework the classical art and philosophy of ancient Greece and Rome. The popes had once been great patrons of Renaissance arts and sciences, but the Counter-Reformation put an end to the Church's liberal leniency in these areas.
15 Further, the Church's new emphasis on religious orthodoxy would soon clash with the emerging scientific revolution. Galileo, with his study of astronomy, found himself at the center of this clash.

Conservative astronomers of Galileo's time, working without telescopes, ascribed without deviation to the ancient theory of geocentricity. This theory of astronomy held that the earth
20 ("geo," as in "geography" or "geology") lay at the center of the solar system, orbited by both the sun and the other planets. Indeed, to the casual observer, it seemed common sense that since the sun "rose" in the morning and "set" at night, it must have circled around the earth. Ancient authorities like Aristotle and the Roman astronomer Ptolemy had championed this viewpoint, and the notion also coincided with the Catholic Church's view of the universe, which placed
25 mankind, God's principal creation, at the center of the cosmos. Buttressed by common sense, the ancient philosophers, and the Church, the geocentric model of the universe seemed secure in its authority. The Ptolemaic theory, however, was not impervious to attack. In the 16th century, astronomers strained to make modern observations fit Ptolemy's geocentric model of the universe.
30 Increasingly complex mathematical systems were necessary to reconcile these new observations with Ptolemy's system of interlocking orbits. Nicholas Copernicus, a Polish astronomer, openly questioned the Ptolemaic system and proposed a heliocentric system in which the planets—including earth—orbited the sun ("helios"). This more mathematically satisfying way of arranging the solar system did not attract many supporters at first, since the
35 available data did not yet support a wholesale abandonment of Ptolemy's system. By the end of the 16th century, however, astronomers like Johannes Kepler (1571–1630) had also begun to embrace Copernicus's theory.

Ultimately, Galileo's telescope struck a fatal blow to the Ptolemaic system. But, in a sense,
40 the telescope was also nearly fatal to Galileo himself. The Catholic Church, desperately trying to hold the Protestant heresy at bay, could not accept a scientific assault on its own theories of the universe. The pressures of the age set in motion a historic confrontation between religion and science, one which would culminate in 1633 when the Church put Galileo on trial, forced
45 him to recant his stated and published scientific beliefs, and put him under permanent house arrest.

The Seven Types of RP Questions

The SAT asks seven types of questions about RPs. These seven types of questions are the *same* for both long RPs and short RPs. So, if you're ready for these seven types, you're ready for every RP question that might appear on the new SAT.

Here's a list of the seven RP question types:

1. Main Idea
2. Attitude or Tone
3. Specific Information
4. Implied Information
5. Themes and Arguments
6. Technique
7. Words in Context

Below, we provide a more thorough explanation of each question type based on sample questions about the Galileo passage above. We provide an explanation of how to answer each question about the Galileo passage that will show you how to answer *all* questions of that type.

1. Main Idea

Main idea questions test your understanding of the entire passage. They don't include specific quotations from the passage. Instead, they ask broad questions that focus on the passage's primary purpose. Unlike themes and arguments questions (question type 5), main idea questions do not concern the author's opinions on the subject—they just focus on the subject or idea itself. Main idea questions cover things such as

- What's the primary purpose of the passage?
- What main idea is the author trying to convey?
- Why did the author write it?

A Sample Main Idea Question

Which of the following best states the main idea of the passage?

(A) Science always conflicts with religion.
(B) Science is vulnerable to outside social forces.
(C) Ideally, scientific theories should reinforce religious doctrine.
(D) Science operates in a vacuum.
(E) Advanced technology is the only route to good scientific theories.

The best way to deal with main idea questions is to come up with a one-sentence summary of the passage. For this passage, you might come up with something like "Galileo's scientific discoveries in particular, and science in general, were affected by the religious and social forces of the time." Once you have the summary, go to the answer choices. In our example question, the answer that best fits the summary is **B**.

But since the passage takes a long time to discuss Galileo's run-ins with the Roman Catholic Church, you might have been tempted by **A**. If you're a bit unsure, a good way to back up your summary is to look at the opening and concluding sentences of the passage, and, if necessary, at the topic sentence of each paragraph (the topic sentence is the first sentence in each paragraph). In the Galileo passage, sentences like the first sentence of this passage—"Galileo Galilei was born in 1564 into a Europe wracked by cultural ferment and religious divisions"—make it clear that the passage is about a scientist in the midst of cultural and religious upheaval. The passage's descriptions of the struggle between the orthodoxy of the Church and the rising scientific revolution help establish the main idea of the passage: that science is vulnerable to outside social forces, **B**.

2. Attitude or Tone

These questions test whether you understand the author's view on the subject. To answer them correctly, you should write down whether the author is for or against his or her subject as you read the passage. It might also be helpful to jot down a few of the points or examples the writer uses to make his or her argument.

The differences in the answer choices for this type of question can be slight. For example, you might have to choose between "irritated" and "enraged." Both of these words suggest that the author has negative sentiments about the topic, but the difference lies in the *intensity* of those feelings. Detecting the words and phrases that convey the intensity of an author's feelings will help you distinguish between different extremes of a similar overall feeling. Determining that a certain topic upsets the author is only the first step. You then need to examine the author's word choice closely to pinpoint the degree of his or her feeling. Is the upset author mildly disturbed? Strongly disapproving? Or enraged? It might help to imagine how the author might sound if he or she read the passage aloud.

If you can't come to a firm decision about the intensity of a feeling, remember that even if all you know is whether the author's tone is positive, negative, or neutral, you'll almost definitely be able to eliminate at least some answer choices and turn the guessing odds in your favor.

A Sample Attitude or Tone Question

The author's tone in this passage can best be described as

(A)   analytical
(B)   disturbed
(C)   skeptical
(D)   dramatic
(E)   reverent

It will help you to first decide whether the author's tone is positive, neutral, or negative, and *then* look at the answers in order to cross off those that don't fit. So, is the Galileo author positive, neutral, or negative? The passage describes an entire time period, covering the different sides, and while it discusses how the Counter-Reformation affected Galileo, it never condemns or praises either the reformation or Galileo. It seeks mainly to describe what happened. So, it's a pretty neutral passage, which means you can eliminate **B** and **C**, since those answer choices are negative, and **E**, since *reverent* ("expressing devotion") is extremely positive. That leaves *dramatic* and *analytical*.

The next step is to ask yourself how the passage would sound if its tone were *dramatic*: It would be full of highs and lows, exclamations and sudden shifts, and it may lurch all over the emotional spectrum. What about if it were *analytical*? It would be a little dry, very informational, with few highs and lows and lots of explanation meant to scrutinize all sides of the problem. Based on that description, analytical sounds like the most accurate way to sum up this writer's tone in the passage. **A** is the correct answer.

3. Specific Information

These questions ask about information that's explicitly stated in the passage. On long RPs, specific information questions usually pinpoint parts of the passage via line numbers or a direct quotation. Very often, specific information questions come in the form of NOT or EXCEPT formats in which you have to choose the one wrong answer out of the five answer choices.

A Sample Specific Information Question

Which of the following was *not* a reason for Martin Luther's attack on the Catholic Church (lines 4–6)?

(A)   pagan elements in its practices
(B)   the amorality of its leadership
(C)   its excessive attention to piety
(D)   its corruption and worldliness
(E)   the political involvement of the popes

There's no reason to ever try to answer this question type without going back to the passage. Take a brief look at the specific lines that the question addresses (in this example, lines 4–6). It's time well spent.

In this passage, lines 4–6 say that Luther attacked the Church for "having become too worldly and politically corrupt and for obscuring the fundamentals of Christianity with pagan elements." That takes out **A**, **B**, **D**, and **E**. so the answer is **C**.

4. Implied Information

Information is "implied" when certain facts, statements, or ideas convey the information but don't declare it outright. Think of these as "suggestion" questions. Implied information questions identify a particular part of the passage and ask you about less obvious information that's "between the lines." To find the correct answer, you may have to deduce what's being said or take a leap of logic. Remember that the leaps the SAT requires you to take are never very vast. Even though implied information questions ask you to reach a bit beyond what the passage states explicitly, they do not require you to think far outside the boundaries of the facts and opinions that the passage overtly contains. Often, you can spot implied information questions when you see words like *context*, *inferred*, *implied*, *indicated*, or *suggested*. Here is a sample of how the SAT phrases implied information questions.

A Sample Implied Information Question

In the second paragraph, the passage implies that during the Renaissance, the Catholic Church

(A)   saw little conflict between its own goals and those of the arts and sciences
(B)   promoted the arts as a way to limit the social influence of scientists
(C)   supported Martin Luther's views on religion and the Church
(D)   had limited interaction with the religious affairs of commoners
(E)   focused on spirituality as opposed to worldly matters

For this kind of question, it's important to come up with your own answer before looking at the answer choices. Outside of the context of the passage, any one of the answer choices might look acceptable to you. It can also be very helpful to think about the main idea of the passage to help you figure out the implied information. Since the author is trying to support a main idea, the information implied in that support will also be associated with the main idea.

This question asks about the Catholic Church during the Renaissance and identifies the second paragraph as the place to look. In that paragraph, it says that during the Renaissance, the Church "was a great patron of the arts and sciences." What does this suggest about the Church during that period? How about this: "The Church liked the arts and sciences during the Renaissance." Now go through the answer choices and look for a match: **A** is by far the best fit and the best answer.

5. Themes and Arguments

The main idea of a passage is its overall purpose. Themes are the recurring concepts that an author uses to establish the main idea. Arguments are the specific perspectives and opinions an author expresses on his or her main idea. Themes and arguments questions test your ability to look at particular parts of a passage and identify the underlying feelings they convey about the main idea. Themes and arguments questions often test your ability to put what the passage says, or how the author feels, into your own words.

The main idea of a passage might be that "the growing rat population is damaging Chicago." Three different themes that an author uses to establish the main idea could be disease, tourism, and city infrastructure. The author's arguments, or specific opinions, could be that the growing rat population has caused the spread of influenza in Chicago, has led to a steep drop in tourism to the city, and threatens to destroy some of the city's most important structures.

A Sample Themes and Arguments Question

Which of the following best explains why the Catholic Church started the Counter-Reformation? (lines 8–10)

(A)   to fight scientific heresy
(B)   to clean out its own ranks
(C)   to reinvigorate artists and intellectuals
(D)   to elect a new pope
(E)   to counter Protestant challenges

The first thing you should do on this type of question is go back to the passage and then come up with your own answer to the question. Once you have this answer in your head, *then* look at the answer choices. If you look at the answer choices before going back to the passage, you're much more likely to make a careless error.

This question tests whether you can follow the flow of argument within the text. More specifically, it tests your ability to differentiate between the causes and effects of the Counter-Reformation. Answers **A**, **B**, and **C** refer to *effects* of the Counter-Reformation, not the causes. But if you were to only look at the answers, any one of these choices might look familiar and therefore tempt you. Avoid temptation. Go back to the passage: "In 1517, Martin Luther, a former monk, attacked Catholicism for having become too worldly and politically corrupt and for obscuring the fundamentals of Christianity with pagan elements. His reforming zeal . . . set in motion the Protestant Reformation and split European Christianity in two. In response, Roman Catholicism steeled itself for battle and launched the Counter-Reformation, which emphasized orthodoxy and fidelity to the true Church." So, your answer to the question of why the Catholic Church started the Counter-Reformation would be something like, "In response to the Protestants and Martin Luther." Answer choice **E** is the best fit and the right answer.

6. Technique

Every author uses certain methods to convey his or her ideas. Technique questions require you to identify the specific literary tool or method the author of the passage uses in a specific part of the passage. This makes technique questions the most likely place for literary terms like *simile* and *metaphor* to appear.

Technique questions can focus on very small units in the passage, such as single words or simple parenthetical statements, or they can target larger units, such as a list, or even the relationship between entire paragraphs.

If you're having trouble figuring out why or how an author is using a particular technique, it can often be helpful to take a step back and look at the technique in light of the author's main point or idea. If you know the main idea, you can often use that information to figure out what an author is trying to accomplish in a particular area of a passage.

A Sample Technique Example

The author's description of Galileo's telescope as having "struck a fatal blow" is an example of a(n)

(A)   simile
(B)   metaphor
(C)   personification
(D)   allusion
(E)   irony

This question tests your knowledge of literary terms—a new subject on the new SAT. (If you're having trouble with literary terms, take some time to look over our literary terms list at the beginning of the Critical Reading section in this book.) In this question, the telescope, an inanimate object, is described as having "struck a fatal blow." In other words, it's been given human qualities, which is the definition of *personification*.

7. Words in Context

These questions present a word or short phrase from the passage and then ask about the meaning of that word in the greater context of the passage. Such questions on long RPs include line numbers that direct you to where the words in the question appear in the passage.

The majority of words-in-context questions look like this:

The word "content" (line 34) is closest in meaning to which of the following words?

Words-in-context questions are a lot like sentence completions, only on these questions, the "blank" comes in the form of a word in quotes. You should try to ignore that word in quotes and imagine it as a blank. In other words, treat words-in-context questions as if they were Sentence Completions.

Why ignore those words in quotes? Because words-in-context questions often have answer choices with words that are indeed correct meanings of the tested word but not the correct meaning of the word *as it appears in the passage*. For example, the question above might contain answer choices such as *satisfied* and *subject*, both of which are correct meanings of the word *content*. But remember that these questions test the word *in context*. By approaching the sentence as if it were a sentence completion, you'll be forced to consider the context of the word in quotes.

A Sample Words in Context Example

1.   The term "ferment" in line 1 most closely means

(A)   alienation
(B)   turmoil
(C)   consolidation
(D)   decomposition
(E)   stagnation

So here's a words-in-context question. Treat it like it's a Sentence Completion: "Galileo Galilei was born in 1564 into a Europe wracked by cultural ---- and religious strife." The sentence is one-way (there are no switch words), so the blank needs to fit with the ideas of "wracked" and "strife," both of which bring up associations with fighting and chaos. See page 5 for Sentence Completion strategy.

LONG RP STRATEGY

By now you know that long and short RPs differ only in length—the questions the SAT asks about them test the same skills. Even so, length makes a big difference when it comes to strategy. Following are the steps you should follow to take on long RPs and their questions. Here's a quick list of all the steps:

Step 1. Force Yourself to Focus
Step 2. Read and Outline the Passage First
Step 3. Answer Specific Questions
Step 4. Answer General Questions

Step 1: Force Yourself to Focus

Almost everyone suffers from DLFD on SAT reading passages: Devastating Loss-of-Focus Disease. You know that hippy phrase, "Free your mind and the rest will follow?" That phrase is a lie. On the SAT, you have to lock up your mind, put it in solitary confinement, and then expect high scores to follow. You have to focus exclusively on the passage before you as if it were the only thing in your life. You must *trick* your mind into being very excited by this prospect. Say to yourself, "I am so excited to read this passage about the history of hot air balloons!"

This seems like a joke, but we're not joking. If you focus on the passage as you would something you really care about, you'll understand and remember much more of the passage. Do whatever you can to engage with the passage, even if it's about sea snails, and try to channel your manufactured passion into better focus and attention to detail. That's what will get you higher scores on reading passages. No joke.

Step 2: Read and Outline the Passage

Read the passage first, paying no attention to the answers. Looking at the answer first may seem like a good idea, but in practice it's just not possible to keep a load of questions in your head while also trying to read the passage.

You should never spend more than *five minutes* reading a long RP. Read the passage quickly, but don't just skim it. We think strategies like reading *only* the first and last sentence of each paragraph do more harm than good. Why? Because speed reading the first time around will force you to go back frequently to the passage when you get to the questions, which will cost you time. Instead, read the entire passage and focus intently on the most important parts of every long RP: The introduction, the conclusion, and the first and last sentences of each paragraph. This will ensure that you are not just reading but *actively* reading.

How to Read the Passage

Don't get bogged down trying to soak up every single fact and detail. Remember, questions that deal with specifics will give you line numbers, so going back to the passage won't be a big deal. You don't have to memorize the passage, you just have to get a solid gist of it.

Read the passage with an awareness of the big-picture questions that RP questions will ask you.

- What is the author's goal in writing the passage?
- What's the author's tone?
- What's the primary argument that the author makes?
- What literary techniques does the author use to convey his or her ideas?

It's also a good idea to take a few seconds after each paragraph to summarize for yourself what you just read and jot it down in your test booklet. This will help you retain the content of each passage and trace the overall structure and feel of the passage.

How to Outline the Passage

When it comes time to answer questions about an RP, having a rough outline of the passage will be very helpful. When we say you should write an outline, we don't mean a thorough kind of outline with bullet points and roman numerals that you'd write for a teacher. We just mean you should keep a rough sketch in the margins of the RP in your test booklet.

Here's how: As you read each RP, keep a shorthand written record of your thoughts on the passage as you read through it. Write down the purpose of each paragraph as you go and jot down ideas about the tone, arguments, and techniques you spot along the way. That way, when you finish reading the passage, you'll already be armed with answers to some of the questions that you know will show up on the test, such as tone, main idea, themes and arguments, and technique. Underline topic sentences, draw in brackets to mark lists of examples that support the main argument, circle important names—mark anything relating to general themes and ideas, the main idea of each paragraph, and other aspects of the passage that strike you as important. This will reinforce what you read as you read it and give you a road map of the passage to use when you go back to answer specific questions.

Step 3: Answer Specific Questions

When you finish the passage, go straight to the questions. Specific questions refer to particular line numbers or paragraphs in the passage. We suggest you tackle these questions before the more general questions because those typically require more thought, time, and attention than specific questions.

Specific questions refer directly to words or lines in the passage. Before going back to the paragraph, articulate to yourself exactly what the question is asking. Don't look at the answers (this will help you avoid being caught by SAT traps). Next, go to the specified area in the passage and read just the few lines before and after it to get a sense of the context. Come up with your own answer to the question, then go back and find the answer that best matches yours.

Step 4: Answer General Questions

You should be able to answer general questions without looking back at the passage. General questions do not refer to specific locations in the passage. Instead, they ask about broad aspects of the passage such as its main idea, tone, and argument. Often the best way to answer general questions like these is to refer to the outline of the passage you made as you read through it. If you've already jotted down notes in your outline on the purpose of each paragraph, the tone, and the overall argument of the passage, you'll be all set to take on general questions with ease.

Your ability to answer general tone and main idea questions without looking back at the passage is also a good gauge of how well you're reading the passage. If you're having trouble with these sorts of questions and have to go back to the passage to answer them, you might be speeding through the passage too quickly or focusing too much on specific information.

CHALLENGED TO A DUAL (PASSAGE)

The new SAT contains one dual passage, which is SAT-speak for two separate passages that are somehow related. When you get to the dual passage, here's what you'll see:

- Italicized introduction
- Passage 1
- Passage 2
- Questions on passage 1
- Questions on passage 2
- Questions that ask you to relate the two passages

The secret to dual passages is: Do *not* follow this order. Instead, treat each passage separately, with the four-step method we just showed you. That results in the following five-step method for dual RPs:

1. Read the introduction and the first passage.
2. Answer the questions about *the first passage only.*

3. Read the second passage.
4. Answer the questions about *the second passage only.*
5. Answer the questions that address both passages together.

Treating the passages separately makes sense for a number of reasons. First, it means that you'll be answering the questions on a particular passage when that passage is freshest in your mind. That will save you time, since you won't have to jump back and forth between questions and passages. Second, it means that you won't get so caught up looking for relationships between the two passages that you'll lose focus on the individual passages. By the time you've dealt with the two passages individually, you'll have naturally built up a strong enough understanding of each passage to be able to answer the questions that ask you to relate the two passages.

These "relating" passages questions usually ask you to compare a variety of aspects of the two passages, such as the main idea of the two passages, individual arguments in each passage, and the tones of each passage. Sometimes questions relating two passages get a bit more creative by asking you to predict how the author of one passage might think about information presented in the other passage.

THE SKINNY ON RP CONTENT

RPs on the new SAT split into two big categories:

- Nonfiction passages (on everything from science to art to history to literature)
- Fiction passages excerpted from literary works

Nonfiction Passages

These are the RPs that you expect to see on the SAT. You know, the ones with a bunch of paragraphs about a Native American tribe, the scientist who invented carbon dating, or a famous Civil War battle. These passages are always nonfiction with no distinct narrative voice. That means they're based on facts and read like newspaper or journal articles. The individual "voice" or identity of the author does not play much of a role in the discussion or the topic at hand in these passages.

None of these passages require you to have any background knowledge in the topics they cover. The passage or passages always contain every bit of information you need to answer the questions correctly. Below, we list a few details about the specific kinds of nonfiction, non-narrative passages you can expect to encounter on the new SAT. But keep in mind that all of these subcategories test similar skills, namely, how well you can understand and evaluate what the passage contains.

Science Passages

Science passages range from discussions or debates about topics in science to descriptions of scientific events throughout history. For example, science subject matter may include a scientist arguing that genetics affect decisions about where people build their cities, a historian describing the disagreements between physicists in the early twentieth century, or an explanation of the earthworm's digestive system. All the science you need to know is presented in the passage—you should not expect to find anything like physics or chemistry formulas in science RPs.

History Passages

History RPs come in two forms: (1) passages taken from history, such as a historical address about an event or situation in society, and (2) passages in which historians write about and interpret history. Questions about history passages tend to focus heavily on your ability to understand the author's argument. History passages also frequently test your understanding of unfamiliar words in context. For example, a question about a passage on the Civil War may ask you to identify the definition of a word like *bayonet* based on the context of the passage.

Literary Criticism Passages

These passages usually discuss one of the following topics: a particular book or writer, a literary movement or trend, or some overarching literary concept. Questions following literary criticism RPs are almost always about the tone of the passage or the writer's point of view or overall opinion. Vocabulary is a dead giveaway of the writer's tone and argument in these passages.

Art Passages

Art passages discuss specific pieces of art, trends in art history, or particular artists. "Art" on the SAT usually means painting, architecture, or music. Art passages might involve the artist speaking about his or her own work, the artist speaking about his or her field in general, a critic discussing a specific work or artist, or a description of some controversy in the art world. Passages about specific artists usually try to locate that artist in the context of broader trends or movements.

Fiction Passages

Fiction is the wildcard that the new SAT has thrown into the long RP mix. *Every* Critical Reading section of the new SAT includes one fiction narrative passage. Fiction passages are very different from other RPs on the test, since they're the product of a writer's imagination. Instead of dealing with arguments or big concepts in science, literature, art, and history, fictional narratives require you to deal with characters, emotions, point of view, and literary style.

This means you have to think a little differently. As you read a fiction passage, think about why the author chose to write what he or she wrote. Why did the writer choose the images described in the passage? What rhetorical device like similes, metaphors, and personification did the author use? What is the tone? What is the writer's relationship to the characters, memories, or events being described? How do the characters feel about each other or about these memories or events?

Don't read too deeply into these passages. It won't ask you for a poetic interpretation or an innovative analysis of a passage. It will only ask you questions that you can answer based on what's right in front of you. That makes the best approach to fiction narrative interpreting only what you read directly in the passage. If you feel like you're stretching for an answer, you're probably not on the right track. Stick to the facts and ideas that the passage itself can support.

Hmmm . . . Have I Read This Before?

The reading passages on the old SAT were excerpts from obscure books that no high school student would ever have read. Using oddball sources helped bolster the test's fairness, since almost nobody would have read the books from which the passages were excerpted (unless you had perchance sat down one Saturday to read *Anook: Tales of an Eskimo Goat Herder*). So, their decision to use *Anook* and others like him made sense.

The new SAT aims to do a better job than the old SAT of mirroring what students actually learn in school. To encourage high schools to align what they teach, the SAT has now decided to use passages from popular works of literature that high school teachers often assign. The new SAT now includes excerpts from books commonly read in high school, like *Animal Farm* and *The Great Gatsby*. Does this mean your Critical Reading score can be dramatically affected by luck? Yes!

What can you do in response to this bizarre change? We've already encouraged you to read as much as you can in anticipation of the SAT, and the change to using popular works as sources only reinforces that advice. It's highly unlikely, however, that you'll have just read the book from which the passage you encounter is excerpted. Nobody knows exactly which books the SAT will use as sources for passages, so trying to read as many books as possible won't be an effective way to prepare for this change. The best thing to do is to continue reading and training yourself to read and think critically. Rather than reading only popular fiction, newspapers, or magazines, it's probably a good idea to start reading some of the classics commonly studied in high school. You can't read them all, of course, but you can read some of the most popular and important titles, which we've listed below. You can also read summaries and commentary on hundreds of literary classics for free online at *SparkNotes.com*. Here are the top twenty SparkNotes literature titles:

- *To Kill a Mockingbird*
- *The Great Gatsby*
- *The Scarlet Letter*
- *The Adventures of Huckleberry Finn*
- *Lord of the Flies*
- *The Catcher in the Rye*
- *The Odyssey*
- *Frankenstein*
- *Great Expectations*
- *The Crucible*
- *A Tale of Two Cities*
- *Heart of Darkness*
- *1984*
- *Of Mice and Men*
- *Brave New World*
- *The Canterbury Tales*
- *Things Fall Apart*
- *Pride and Prejudice*
- *Jane Eyre*
- *Fahrenheit 451*

THE SHORT OF IT

SHORT READING PASSAGE QUESTIONS ARE LIKE THE LONG-LOST little brother of long RPs. They're a new addition to the SAT family, but they've got the same basic makeup as their older, longer siblings. Short RPs test the same skills and cover the same basic categories of science, literature, art, history, and narrative as long RPs. They even have the same instructions as long RPs. But there is one big difference: They're shorter. And that's enough to change your whole strategy, because it means you can read short RPs word for word.

WHAT SHORT READING PASSAGES LOOK LIKE

Short RPs are about 100 words long and are followed by just two questions. Short RP questions are just like long RP questions. Every question fits into one of the seven categories we covered for long RPs:

1. Main Idea
2. Attitude or Tone
3. Specific Information
4. Implied Information
5. Themes and Arguments
6. Technique
7. Words in Context

A Complete Short RP Example

Here's a sample short RP, complete with two questions. Read the passage and the questions straight through. Then we'll go over strategies for approaching short RPs like this one, including an explanation of how to answer the two questions about this passage using our four-step short RP strategy.

Airplanes are such a common form of travel that it's easy to forget just how recently they were invented. Today, even a person in the middle of nowhere would not be surprised to see a plane in the sky. But before the Wright brothers flew their plane at Kitty Hawk, North Carolina, in 1910, most scientists thought flight by heavier-than-air machines would never be achieved. Never. In fact, the word "airplane" didn't come into common usage until after 1945.

1. The reference to the "person in the middle of nowhere" primarily serves to

(A) introduce a new argument
(B) challenge common beliefs
(C) highlight the limitations of an accepted idea
(D) question modern morals
(E) indicate the scope of a change

2. The author of the passage would most likely agree with each of the following statements EXCEPT

(A) airplanes are a relatively recent innovation
(B) the Wright brothers took the first airplane flight
(C) air travel remains the privilege of the elite
(D) the word "airplane" was rarely used in the early twentieth century
(E) airplanes can be seen almost anywhere

SHORT RP STRATEGY

For long RPs, we advised you to read the entire passage, make a sketchy outline, *then* check out the questions. We suggested that you follow those steps in that order because it'd be impossible to keep an 800-word passage and eight to thirteen questions in your head.

But short RPs are short and have just two questions. That means you *can* comfortably fit the entire passage and the two questions in your head. It also means you don't have to worry about keeping an outline, since you're dealing with only one paragraph. The change in the length of the passage therefore flips your whole strategy on its head: You should read the questions *before* you read the passage. That way, you'll have the *exact* questions you need to answer in mind as you read the passage.

Step 1. Read the two questions but *not* the answer choices.

Step 2. Read the passage, with special focus on answering the two questions.

Step 3. Come up with answers for the two questions in your own words.

Step 4. Match your answer to the correct answer.

Now let's see what happens when we apply this method to the two questions from our sample short RP.

Sample Short RP Answers and Explanations

Here's the first question again:

1. The reference to the "person in the middle of nowhere" primarily serves to

    (A) introduce a new argument
    (B) challenge common beliefs
    (C) highlight the limitations of an accepted idea
    (D) question modern morals
    (E) indicate the scope of a change

Let's say you ignore our four-step method and read through this passage, skipping step 1. You'd have no clue what the questions are, so you'd just breeze by the phrase about the "person in the middle of nowhere." Then you'd get to the first question and would have to go back to reread the entire sentence containing the "person in the middle of nowhere" phrase, wasting precious time.

Instead, if you had followed step 1 and read the questions first, you'd know what you were looking for. You'd then read the passage and keep an eye out for that particular phrase (step 2). You'd notice that the phrase "not even a person in the middle of nowhere would be surprised to see a plane in the sky" emphasizes how common airplanes are now, and it draws a contrast to a hundred years ago when scientists did not believe such flight was possible. That means the author uses that phrase to point out that today, no one, anywhere would be surprised to see a plane in the sky. That's your version of the answer to this technique question (step 3). Now take a look at the real answer choices and try to find one that matches yours closely (step 4). **E** matches almost perfectly. The author uses the reference to the "person in the middle of nowhere" to indicate the scope of the change from the days when airplanes were foreign to almost everyone.

Now, for the second question from the sample passage:

2. The author of the passage would most likely agree with each of the following statements EXCEPT

    (A) airplanes are a relatively recent innovation
    (B) the Wright brothers took the first airplane flight
    (C) air travel remains the privilege of the elite
    (D) the word "airplane" was rarely used in the early twentieth century
    (E) airplanes can be seen almost anywhere

Reading the questions first (step 1) can save you lots of time on EXCEPT questions. This themes and arguments question asks you to find the statement that the author would *not* agree with, so as you read the passage with the question in mind, you can check off the statements that the passage confirms as you read. Notice that on EXCEPT questions like this one, you have to read the answer choices first as well, since the question alone does not give you enough information to work with as you read the passage (step 2). Using this method will actually allow you to skip step 3 and 4, since the answer will be the only unchecked answer choice that remains after you've read the passage and checked off the statements with which the author would agree.

The author's main argument in this passage is that air travel has become entirely commonplace even though the invention of flight only happened one hundred years ago. You can knock out **A**, since the author would certainly agree that air travel is a recent invention. Check off **B** since the author references the Wright brothers' famous first flight directly in the passage. **D** and **E** can get checks too, because they cover material that the author clearly supports in the passage: that airplanes can be seen even in the middle of nowhere and that the word *airplane* only came into common usage recently. Only **C** stands out as directly against the author's main theme and argument: rather than remaining exclusively for the wealthy, air travel can now be enjoyed by almost anyone. After having read the passage and checked off answer choices as you read, only **C** would remain, and that's the correct answer.

CHALLENGED TO A (SHORT) DUAL

Dual short RPs present you with *two* 100-word passages, and then *four* questions. The first question deals with the first passage, the second covers the second passage, and the last two questions cover the relationship between the passages.

As with the long dual passage, you should treat each short dual passage individually:

1. Read the question about the first passage, and then read the first passage.
2. Come up with your own answer and compare it to the actual answer choices in the question about the first passage.
3. Read the question about the second passage, then read the second passage. Think about how the second passage relates to the first.
4. Come up with your own answer and compare it to the actual answer choices in the question about the second passage.
5. Answer the questions that address both passages together.

By the time you get to step 5, you'll be so familiar with the passages that you won't have to look back at them to answer the two questions that ask you to relate them.

Sample Short Dual RP

Here are two related brief passages followed by four questions: two that treat the passages together and two that treat them individually.

Few things in life are as rewarding and fulfilling as owning a pet. Whether it's a dog, cat, bird, or fish, the appeal is the same—years of fun and unconditional love. Indeed, pets can actually satisfy many of the things people crave most: companionship, communication, loyalty, and plenty of amusement. Perhaps that's why pets are so popular among the elderly and people who live alone. As human relationships grow more complex with each new technological gadget, the simple bond between a pet and its owner offers a refreshing and comforting reprieve.

In addition to protesting reprehensible practices like fur trapping and animal testing, animal rights groups have begun to attack owners of cats and dogs for keeping animals "imprisoned" in the home. Finally, these groups have started to make the justified comparison of owning a pet to keeping a domesticated animal like a sheep or a cow. Both pet ownership and domestication of animals stem from the same cruel source: human selfishness. No animal should be kept confined solely for the benefit of human beings, whether that benefit comes in the form of meat, leather, or the companionship of a pet.

Sample Dual Short RP Questions and Explanations

1. How might you sum up the author's main idea in the first passage?

    (A) Owning a pet is cruel and unfair.
    (B) Pets should always be leashed.
    (C) Pet ownership has profound rewards.
    (D) Pet ownership is technologically advanced.
    (E) Pets need new forms of communication.

2. The word "reprehensible" in the second passage most nearly means

    (A) demoralizing
    (B) invigorating
    (C) restorative
    (D) disgraceful
    (E) delightful

3. Based on information in these two passages, the authors disagree about whether

    (A) animals should be kept as pets
    (B) pets are beneficial for humans
    (C) fur trapping should be illegal
    (D) kennel conditions should be reformed
    (E) human beings are inherently selfish

4. Which words among the pairs below best describe the tone of the first passage and of the second passage, respectively?

    (A) alarmed and disengaged
    (B) enthusiastic and critical
    (C) despondent and exuberant
    (D) elated and enervated
    (E) wary and disapproving

Explanations

1. **C**

Step 1 tells you to read this question before reading the first passage, since it's specifically about the first passage. You then know to think about coming up with your own quick description of the main idea of the first passage as you read. This author strongly supports pet ownership because it rewards pet owners with years of fun and love. So, that's your answer to describe main idea of the passage.

Now take a look at the actual answer choices and look for a description of the passage's main idea that comes closest to your description of the joys of pet ownerships (step 2). **A** is out because it describes having a pet as "cruel" and "unfair." **B**, **D**, and **E** are all SAT traps because each mentions something vaguely mentioned in the passage (leashes, technological innovations, and communication), but none captures the main idea. Only **C** matches the answer you generated to describe the main idea: Owning a pet brings profound, or deep, rewards to pet owners. **C** is the correct answer.

2. **D**

Step 3 tells you to read the question(s) about the second passage *before* reading the second passage. You'd then know to pay close attention as you read the passage to the sentence with the word *reprehensible* so you don't have to go back and find it later.

And there it is, right in the first sentence. Since this is a words-in-context question, treat it like a Sentence Completion and use the rest of the paragraph to help you fill in the blank with your own answer. The sentence is: "In addition to protesting ---- practices like fur trapping and animal testing, animal rights groups have begun to attack owners of cats and dogs for keeping animals 'imprisoned' in the home." The switch words *in addition to* show that the sentence is one-way: The animal rights groups are acting consistently. And it's clear from the rest of the passage that the writer is really, really against pet ownership. So, it would seem that the blank must be filled with an extremely negative word like *awful*.

You can throw out answers **B**, **C**, and **E**, because each is a positive word. That leaves *demoralizing* and *disgraceful*. These two words are both negative, but *demoralizing* means "negatively affecting morale," which isn't quite strong enough to reflect this writer's anger about the mistreatment of animals. So the answer is **D**.

3.   **A**

By the time you get to dual passage questions that ask about both passages together, you will have already read and answered specific questions about both passages. That means you don't need to read them again and can dive right in to generating your own answers and comparing them to the actual answer choices.

This question asks about what the authors of the two passage disagree about. The divergent views of the authors of these two passages are quite clear: One supports pet ownership enthusiastically and one objects to it strongly. Let's say that's the answer you generate on your own. Now let's see which answer choice matches it. Since you've established that the question of whether "animals should be kept as pets" is the core of their disagreement, **A** is the correct answer.

B is incorrect because while the first passage would agree with the statement, the second passage does not disagree; it just says that the question of whether having a pet is beneficial for the human is not the issue. **C** is an SAT trap. The SAT wants you to see "fur trapping," which the second passage mentions briefly, and pick that answer. But the first author does not mention fur trapping at all, so it is definitely not the main issue here. Cut **C**. Neither passage mentions kennels, so eliminate **D**. **E** is incorrect because only the author of the second passage would explicitly agree with the sentiment that human beings are selfish.

4.   **B**

This question asks about the tone of the two passages. Since you've read both passages thoroughly already, generate your own answer and compare it to the real answer choices.

What words might you already have in mind to describe the tone of these two passages? The first is positive, encouraging, and excited about the prospect of owning a pet. The second is negative, disapproving, and concerned about pet ownership in general. With that in mind, you should be able to select **B** as correct: The first passage is *enthusiastic* in tone, whereas the second is *critical*.

Now, try your hand at the seven practice sets that follow.

PRACTICE SET 1: LONG READING PASSAGE— FICTION

<u>Questions 1–9</u> refer to the passage below.

The following passage is from a 2003 novel about a young woman named Angela who at age eight left China with her family to move to San Francisco.

Our parents had known each other in China; we'd even taken the same boat to America. However, within five years of our arrival in San Francisco, Norman and I had become strangers. Relatives already established in the city helped Norman's parents assimilate. Within a year, they had not only learned English, but had also become real
5 estate moguls. I learned all this from the Chinese American gossip machine that constantly tabulated every family's level of success. The machine judged my family lacking. My parents ran a grocery store and, unlike Norman's family, gravitated to the immigrant subculture. They never learned English, but they respected that I tamed that beast of a language. I was my parents' communication link with the "outside
10 world."

My parents denied themselves in order to ensure that I could attend Baywood, a top private high school. That was where Norman and I crossed paths again. However much my relative mastery of English had elevated my status at home, at Baywood I remained a shy and brainy outsider. Norman was very popular: he played football and was elected
15 class president. He and gorgeous Judy Kim were named King and Queen of the Winter Ball; their portrait adorned every available bulletin board. I scoffed at the celebrity silently. Back then, I did everything silently. Compared to Norman, who had already achieved the American teenage ideal, I was anonymous. From the sidelines I observed his triumphs with barely acknowledged envy.

20 In May of our freshman year, Norman approached me after our chemistry class.

"Hey, Angela," he said as my heart leapt into my throat. "I missed class a couple of days ago. Can I copy your notes?"

"Sure," I said. I was horrified to find myself blushing.

We soon became study buddies. It was all business—no small talk beyond the
25 necessary niceties. But the hours we piled up studying together generated an unspoken mutual respect and an unacknowledged intimacy. Judy noticed this and took an increasing dislike to me. This relationship continued throughout high school.

One day in eleventh grade, without looking up from the math problem he was working on, Norman asked: "What schools are you applying to?"

30 It was the first time he had shown any real personal interest in me. "Berkeley, if I'm lucky," I said.

"You could probably get in anywhere."

"What do you mean?"

He looked up from his math problem and met my gaze.

35 "Berkeley is just across the bay. Don't you want to experience something new for once? I'm applying to schools back East," he said. "You should, too."

Not for the first time, an exciting vision of ivy-covered walls and perhaps even a new identity swept over me and was almost immediately subsumed by a wave of guilt.

"But what about my parents?"

40 "But what about *you*?"

Norman had broken a taboo. I launched into a self-righteous refutation of the possibility he had dared to voice. I told him that even though *I* wasn't popular and *my* family wasn't as successful as his, *I* at least hadn't forgotten that it was my parents who had brought me here and who had struggled so much for me. How could I make them

45 unhappy?

Norman had expected this outburst. He smiled. "We're not so different, you know. We started out in the same boat. Now we're in the same boat again." He laughed. "We've always been in the same boat. Our parents might be kind of different, but they want us to succeed and be happy."

50 "You're so American," I said in a tone hovering between approval and reproach. "You're not even worried about leaving your parents to go to school back East."

"That's not what being American means," he insisted.

"Well, what does it mean, then?" I demanded. Surely, I, and not this superficial football player who needed my academic help, knew what it meant to be American. That

55 very day I had received an A on my American History term paper.

"It means, Angela," he said gently, "that our parents brought us here so we could have the freedom to figure out *for ourselves* what to do with our lives."

He smiled at my speechlessness and then returned to his math problem.

Without looking up from his notebook, he said, "If I can decide to go to school back

60 East, so can you."

1. What is the purpose of the information in the first sentence?

   (A) to show Angela and Norman's similar histories so as to emphasize their current differences
   (B) to emphasize that both Angela and Norman have come a long way since their childhoods in China
   (C) to let the reader know that Angela came from a poor family that could not afford to fly to America
   (D) to make the reader think that Norman and Angela will inevitably become friends
   (E) to let the reader see how highly Angela values her family's history

2. The word "tabulated" in line 6 emphasizes that

   (A) the other Chinese immigrants were very aware of who was succeeding in a material way and who was not
   (B) Angela's neighbors calculated the exact amount of money her family was earning
   (C) Norman's family checked the prices of everything they owned
   (D) Angela lived in a poor section of San Francisco
   (E) Angela was determined to earn more money than Norman

3. The use of italics in line 40 serves to emphasize

   (A) Norman's unrealistic desire to go to school outside of California
   (B) Norman's idealistic goals as contrasted with Angela's lack of ambition
   (C) Norman's concern that Angela has not thought about her own educational desires
   (D) the small chance that Angela will accomplish her dreams
   (E) the degree to which Angela has undermined her potential

4. Angela's response in lines 41–45 reveals that she

   (A) wants Norman to be impressed with her
   (B) is afraid to express her true emotions
   (C) stubbornly wants to attend Berkeley
   (D) is unable to reveal her true ambitions to Norman
   (E) has consistently adopted her parents' happiness as her own

5.   In line 50, Angela uses the word "American" to differentiate between

    (A) concern for the future and fear of failure
    (B) personal ambition and responsibility to one's parents
    (C) imagination and conservatism
    (D) duty to family and duty to friends
    (E) love for adventure and love for travel

6.   In lines 54–55, Angela mentions her A on her history paper in order to

    (A) suggest that she assumes that she knows the definition of "American" better than Norman
    (B) emphasize the high quality of her education
    (C) highlight the irony of knowing the textbook definition of a term versus a real-life meaning
    (D) remind herself that she has spent many years mastering the English language
    (E) strengthen her resolve to go to school in Berkeley instead of the East Coast

7.   Norman's statement in lines 56–57 primarily shows him to be

    (A) selfish in his desires to achieve success
    (B) ambitious in a manner Angela had not considered for herself
    (C) dismissive of his parents' hopes for his future
    (D) secretly hoping to corrupt Angela's future plans
    (E) arrogant in overestimating his abilities

8.   Throughout the passage, the main focus is on

    (A) the awkwardness Angela feels knowing that Norman already has a girlfriend
    (B) Angela's ambition to do well in school and get into a good college
    (C) the challenges Angela faces living in America while feeling like an outsider
    (D) Angela's excitement over getting an A on her history term paper
    (E) how personal ambition is the key to getting ahead in America

9.   From details in the passage, it is clear that

    (A) Angela went ahead with her plan to attend Berkeley
    (B) Angela grew to be more outspoken
    (C) Norman went on to play football in college
    (D) Angela decided to go to college back East
    (E) Angela majored in math at college

ANSWERS & EXPLANATIONS

1.   **A**

The first sentence informs the reader that Angela's parents and Norman's parents knew each other in China and that the two young people came across on the same boat. This common history contrasts with and thereby draws attention to their very different personalities and very different attitudes toward their family responsibilities and personal ambitions: Norman is popular and wants to explore America, while Angela is shy and wants to stay close to home. These differences provide the passage with its tension and interest. The other answers all offer details that may be true to a certain extent, but none of which is as important to the passage as a whole.

2.   **A**

The word *tabulated* appears in the passage to express what the "Chinese American gossip machine" does with regard to "every family's success," and from the context of the passage it is clear that this involves keeping a record of that success and comparing it to the success of other Chinese American families, things for which one might use a table or chart. Choice **B** is tempting since the word *tabulated* sounds like and is occasionally used to mean "calculated," but it is clear that in this context comparisons of status are more germane than exact calculations of salaries.

3. **C**

Angela responds to Norman's suggestion that she think about applying to East Coast colleges with the question "What about my parents?" because she thinks it would be wrong to move far away from her mother and father. Norman, however, thinks it would be worse for Angela to put concern for her parents ahead of her own educational ambitions, and the word *you* is italicized to express his desire that Angela should consider her own interests first.

4. **E**

Angela's answer to Norman's question "What about *you*?" hinges on the idea that she has not forgotten that her parents brought her to America and provided her with the opportunity to excel there. As a result, she feels that she can be happy if and only if her parents are happy. This is clearly articulated by the final part of her response: "How could I make them unhappy?"

5. **B**

Angela clarifies her remark that Norman is "so American" by telling him, "You're not even worried about leaving your parents to go to school back East." Angela is shocked that Norman would put his personal ambition (to attend an Eastern college) before his responsibilities to his parents (which would entail going to school close to their home on the West Coast).

6. **A**

Angela has accused Norman of being "so American" for not worrying about leaving his parents behind to attend college on the East Coast, and he has replied by challenging her definition of "being American." Angela mentions the high grade she received on her paper to suggest that her definition *has* to be better than Norman's since she considers herself to be smarter than he. Choice **B** is attractive since getting an A on a paper seems to relate to the idea of being well educated, but Angela is not concerned with the quality of the education she has received, only the fact that she considers herself intellectually superior to Norman. Similarly, choice **C** is tempting because the word "textbook" seems to fit with a school grade, but Angela's comment is not concerned with the distinctions between textbook and real-life definitions. Rather, it shows that she assumes herself to be intellectually superior to her study-buddy, Norman.

7. **B**

Norman's statement expresses his opinion that his parents want him to do whatever he thinks is best for himself and the fact that he is keen to embrace such freedom. This attitude is in marked contrast to Angela's, which only extends to personal ambitions that coincide with her parents' interests. Choice **A** is tempting since at the time the story takes place, Angela clearly thinks such self-interest is selfish. But this is not Norman's belief. Choice **C** is attractive for the same reason. Choice **D** is too extreme—Norman is trying to help Angela, as Angela has helped him with his studies.

8. **C**

The main idea of the first paragraph is that Angela's family never assimilated into American culture the way Norman's did, and was even judged as insufficient by the "Chinese American gossip machine." In the second paragraph, the reader learns that Angela felt like an outsider at high school, despite her success in learning English. Finally, in the conversation with Norman, Angela realizes that her study partner may know more about what it means to be American, regardless of the A she got on her American History paper, and that she has never considered taking advantage of the freedom to choose that her parents provided her by bringing her to America. Throughout the passage, Angela feels that she is alienated from her surroundings in one way or another. The other choices are details of the passage, or distortions of those details.

9.   **B**

Remember, *Angela*—an older, wiser Angela—is the narrator. In lines 20–21, Angela remarks that "back then, I did everything silently." The phrase *back then* indicates that doing everything silently is something Angela overcame later in life and that she became more outspoken. Although Norman's suggestion that she could attend an Eastern college clearly made an impact on Angela, it is not clear from the passage whether she decided to follow up on this idea or stick with her plan to attend Berkeley, so answers **A** and **D** are incorrect. There is no indication that Angela went on to major in math or that Norman continued to play football, so answers **C** and **E** are incorrect.

the
new SAT
Critical
Reading
Workbook

PRACTICE SET 2: DUAL READING PASSAGE— SCIENCE

the
new SAT
Critical
Reading
Workbook

Directions: *The passages below are followed by questions based on the content of the passages and the relationship between the two passages. Answer the questions on the basis of what the passage* <u>states</u> *or* <u>implies</u> *and on any introductory material provided.*

<u>Questions 1–12</u> refer to the following pair of passages.

On January 14, 2004, President Bush announced a reorganization of NASA resources to make a manned mission to Mars the agency's primary goal. This announcement reignited a long-smoldering debate on manned space travel. These passages, adapted from recently published articles, discuss the advisability of further American investment in manned space travel.

Passage 1

The popularity of manned space flight stems from a peculiar mixture of American ideals buried deep in the national consciousness. Can-do optimism and engineering know-how combine with a New Frontier to provide something quasi-religious: the chance to be born again by ascending to the heavens. Unprecedented material benefits—the storied "spin-offs" that we're always promised—will doubtlessly emanate from this noble effort that will unify our fractious country. Marshalling America's

5   techno-scientific expertise for a Pilgrimage into space will allow us to re-enact our national origins and renew our appointed role: to create a shining City on a Hill in a New World that presents the last best hope of mankind. Thus, manned space flight reconciles seemingly contradictory aspects of the national identity: nostalgic and forward-looking, religious and scientific, spiritual and material.

10   Only through the sobering examination of the costs and benefits of manned space flight can the effect of so seductively romantic a brew be shaken off. Should we spend hundreds of billions of dollars on, say, a mission to Mars when we face crushing problems such as poverty, terrorism, and global warming? The likely benefits of manned space flight had better be staggering in the face of the opportunity costs* of not

15   directly investing in problems such as these.

        Thus, I would like to discuss a non-romantic argument often put forth in favor of manned space flight. Enthusiasts claim that space-based scientific research is both invaluable and impossible to replicate on Earth. There is little proof for this claim. For example, *Mir*, the now-defunct space station, yielded no scientific breakthroughs

20   commensurate with its cost. In one experiment, scientists concluded that plants did not grow well in space. Clearly, this bit of information would be invaluable only to astronauts. Furthermore, a reexamination of this experiment found that plant growth had been stunted for quite mundane and well-understood reasons. Ethylene, a gas long known to be released by plants, had accumulated in the enclosure and inhibited

25   growth. So much for invaluable groundbreaking advances. As for important research

* An "opportunity cost" is a comparison between the likely return on one investment and the likely return on another.

that can't be accomplished on Earth, it is often argued that the only way to study the long-term effects of zero-gravity on the human body is in space. This argument carries weight only for those already committed to manned space flight. But as an independent argument *for* manned space flight, this argument is circular: we must have manned space flight to understand the long-term effects of zero-gravity in order to have more manned space flight.

A sober cost/benefit analysis shows that robotic space exploration trumps manned space flight. Robots have proven to be remarkably effective at exploring our solar system. Their scientific impact is ubiquitously acknowledged. In terms of financial and human cost, robot expeditions are far cheaper to mount.

The circularity of even seemingly non-romantic arguments for manned space flight belies the fundamental romanticism of its supporters. Doubtlessly unaware of the ingredients in the seductive brew noted above, enthusiasts support manned space flight because they think it would be really fun and exciting. Being an American, I can understand this. I, too, yearn for adventures on alien shores. But even though it would be really fun and exciting to deplete all my savings on a year-long adventure on merely Mediterranean shores, as an adult I know that I have more pressing, if less enticing, claims on my resources. Those who argue for manned space flight do so out of romantic, escapist, and childlike notions that they should outgrow.

Passage 2

The orbiting astronaut looks down on his home and grasps both its fragility and the pettiness of our mundane conflicts. How trite! How dare we spend vast sums on manned space flight when six billion of us live in the midst of conflicts and problems, which, while perhaps "petty" from a God's-eye view, threaten the future of our civilization and species? Furthermore, the oft-made assertion that manned space experiments have yielded critical advances either directly or indirectly is arguable at best.

So goes the fashionable critique of manned space travel. However, rather than cynically dismiss the astronaut's now proverbial reaction to seeing the Earth from on high, I propose that we consider the potential benefits that this change in perspective would have on real-world problems were it only spread more widely. Moreover, equally intangible "romantic" impulses to explore should not be thrown aside so lightly. Motivation matters. Where would we be today if Christopher Columbus had not embarked on his "folly" to open a western passage to the East? Beneficial unintended consequences—or, "spin-offs"—are real and pre-date the moon shot. Columbus, in fact, failed to open a new trade route to the East, but he did find two continents previously unknown to his contemporaries in Europe, Asia, and Africa. While clearly not entirely beneficial—especially for the millions of Native Americans felled by Old-World diseases or conquistadors' muskets—Columbus' discovery nevertheless made great things possible, such as the United States.

Rather than retreat in embarrassment from the charge of "romanticism," we should embrace it. The case for manned space flight should rest explicitly upon the rejuvenating and unifying potential the effort provides our troubled world. In particular, we should cease insisting that immensely important scientific discoveries are imminent and inevitable. While this almost certainly is the case, we really don't need *manned* space flight to yield scientific discoveries; robots do very well for that purpose. Moreover, the real-world benefits of intangible inspiration are not limited to a welcome and fruitful change in perspective. How many young people would rush into the sciences if a full-scale global effort in manned space flight—a mission to Mars is the obvious choice—were launched? How beneficial would the consequences of the requisite and unprecedented international cooperation be for the grave issues that face our species here on Earth?

Rather than promise dubious economic boons when we're labeled "escapist," we should explicitly state the possibility that we have already failed on this planet and that space is our only long-term option. Most scientists agree that we are already dangerously close to Earth's carrying capacity. Surely, within the half-century or so it would take to truly conquer manned space flight, we will be that much closer to a nightmare of ecological or societal collapse. Doesn't the likely prospect of global collapse in itself represent the most massive opportunity cost possible for *not* investing heavily in manned space flight? It's

40 at the very least arguable that the new frontier of the Americas gave rise to a kind of society whose ideals truly are the last best hope of mankind. Wouldn't the new frontier of space bestow another opportunity for fruitful experiments in enlightened government? I maintain that we cannot afford to throw aside the undeniable romantic appeal that a global effort to put man in space would engender. Our civilization will

45 need all the help it can get to survive this century. I can think of no argument for manned space flight more unromantic than that.

1. Which of the following, if true, would most clearly STRENGTHEN the assertion in Passage 1 about science experiments conducted in space (lines 20–25)?

    (A) Many of the recent developments in gene therapy are directly attributed to experiments conducted on *Mir*.
    (B) Recent reports have questioned the objectivity of the critics of the *Mir* program.
    (C) A full report on all experiments conducted in space has yet to be evaluated.
    (D) A list of the 100 most important scientific discoveries since the beginning of manned space travel yielded none based on experiments conducted in space.
    (E) Many of the experiments conducted in space are highly technical, and not easily accessible to the layman.

2. With which of the following statements would the author of Passage 1 be LEAST likely to agree?

    (A) When considering whether an investment is worthwhile, the likely benefits of that investment should be weighed against the likely benefits of a similar investment in another venture.
    (B) The benefits of manned space missions do not outweigh the benefits of robotic space missions to a degree significant enough to justify the higher cost of the former.
    (C) The strong support for manned space missions among Americans is surprising given the spirituality of the American people.
    (D) It is part of the American character to be attracted by the idea of experiencing exciting adventures in new territories.
    (E) Part of becoming an adult is coming to recognize that the potential benefits of any venture must be weighed against the costs.

3. In the context of lines 30–33 of Passage 1, the reference to "circular" serves to

    (A) outline the path which astronauts take when in orbit
    (B) emphasize that arguments which support sending humans into space are self-serving
    (C) illustrate the accuracy needed to gauge an astronaut's health in space
    (D) demonstrate the progress that has been made in helping humans to adapt to the demands of space
    (E) refute the argument that space travel is costly and even unnecessary

4. In line 34 of Passage 1, "trumps" most nearly means

    (A) devises
    (B) suits
    (C) duplicates
    (D) outperforms
    (E) defrauds

5.   According to Passage 2, the argument that people should not go into space is

(A) harmlessly entertaining
(B) unjustly scornful
(C) logically flawed
(D) astutely argued
(E) unnecessarily complicated

6.   The author of Passage 2 begins by describing an astronaut's view from space in order to

(A) emphasize that the astronaut is a kind of national hero
(B) show how overly simplistic things look in space
(C) prepare the reader for the idea that new perspectives can be important
(D) warn the reader against adopting an overly romantic notion of space travel
(E) prove that environmental problems are so severe that their effects can be seen
        from space

7.   The word "fashionable" in line 8 of Passage 2 most nearly means

(A) flattering
(B) apparent
(C) wholesome
(D) trendy
(E) conspicuous

8.   Which of the following strategies for arguing in favor of manned space missions would the
     author of Passage 2 be MOST likely to favor?

(A) emphasizing the importance of scientific experiments conducted in space
(B) showing the benefits of traveling to Mars
(C) emphasizing the way it will nurture and inspire positive sentiments in the people
        back on Earth
(D) proving precisely what discoveries lie in wait for us in space
(E) eliminating the danger of manned space travel

9.   Which of the following most accurately describes the last paragraph of Passage 2 in relation to
     arguments in Passage 1?

(A) The author of Passage 2 proposes a new argument and revives an argument
        dismissed in Passage 1.
(B) The author of Passage 2 predicts a future series of events also considered in
        Passage 1.
(C) The author of Passage 2 examines an idea from Passage 1 and disputes the figures
        offered in support.
(D) The author of Passage 2 asserts a viewpoint shared by the author of Passage 1 by
        offering up historical evidence.
(E) The author of Passage 2 reconciles his point of view with the author of Passage 1.

10. In each passage, the author assumes that the efficacy of scientific experiments conducted in
     space is

(A) useful only if carefully monitored by a mirror crew on the ground
(B) called into question only by the most cynical of observers
(C) tragically underutilized by the most talented scientists
(D) only justifiable under certain circumstances
(E) not enough to justify manned space flight

11. The passages differ in their evaluation of manned space flight in that Passage 1 claims that

    (A) space enthusiasts ultimately want to go to the moon for romantic notions

    (B) propagandists have falsified the data of scientific experiments to justify their continued use

    (C) the only real benefits of manned space travel could be achieved less expensively with robotic space exploration

    (D) Christopher Columbus had a specific goal in mind when he set off on his journey

    (E) the only way to understand the long-term impact of space travel on the body is to engage in manned space flights

12. Both passages are primarily concerned with

    (A) the poor planning of current space missions

    (B) the future of manned space flight

    (C) the eventuality of going to Mars

    (D) the best way to improve the space program

    (E) the introduction of more math and science into the school curriculum

ANSWERS & EXPLANATIONS

1. **D**

Passage 1 asserts that scientific experiments conducted in space do not yield results important enough to offset their costs, so the correct answer will offer an argument supporting this idea. If it were true that none of the 100 most important scientific discoveries since the beginning of manned space travel was conducted in space, this fact would certainly strengthen the position presented in the first passage. The other answers are incorrect because they all offer facts that, if true, would weaken the claim that scientific experiments conducted in space are not worth their costs.

2. **C**

In lines 2–5, the author of Passage 1 asserts that the idea of sending people into space to explore new frontiers is "quasi-religious" and appeals to the desire to be born again in the heavens; the author seems convinced that the spirituality of Americans is one of the driving forces behind support for the space program. The other answers all offer statements with which the author of Passage 1 would certainly agree, given details and arguments in the passage.

3. **B**

In the third paragraph, the author of Passage 1 shows how the experiments performed aboard the *Mir* space station yielded findings that can only be of use in future manned space missions. In other words, one of the main arguments used to support the continuation of manned missions is based on the assumption that such a continuation will be granted. The argument is self-serving because it essentially says that manned space missions are necessary because manned space missions require research performed on manned space missions.

4. **D**

In the context of the passage, the word *trumps* is being used to describe the way robotic space exploration is more effective than or *outperforms* manned space flight. None of the words offered in the other answer choices makes sense in the context of the passage. **A** and **E** offer clearly nonsensical definitions. **B**, *suits*, does not make sense since robotic and manned space flights are alternatives to one another—a mission is either robotic *or* manned, so one cannot *suit* the other. **C** is more logical, but it would not be accurate to say that robotic space missions *duplicate* manned ones since the author has just asserted that the scientific accomplishments

of the former are universally recognized while those of the latter are only important to astronauts.

5. B

The abrasive language the author uses to articulate the argument against manned space travel ("How trite! How dare we...?"), and the fact that the reader is cautioned against "cynically" dismissing the astronaut's perspective indicate that this argument is regarded as being *unjustly scornful.* **C**, *logically flawed,* is tempting, but Passage 2 disputes the logic against manned space travel showing that supposedly "romantic" arguments in favor of it are actually morbidly hard-headed: "Our civilization will need all the help it can get to survive this cen-tury. I can think of no argument for manned space flight more unromantic than that." There is no evidence to suggest that any of the assessments offered by the other answer choices is accurate.

6. C

In the second paragraph, the author expresses the idea that the astronaut's experience of see-ing the Earth from space grants a new perspective on earthly affairs that might be beneficial if it were spread more widely across the population. **B** and **D** are both tempting because within the first paragraph it appears that the author is criticizing the importance people attach to the astronaut's unique view of the world. Reading the paragraph in the context of the entire pas-sage reveals that the author is writing ironically, however, and is actually objecting to the way people tend to scoff at this enlightening experience.

7. D

The word *fashionable* is applied to the prevailing view of manned space travel against which the author of Passage 2 is arguing. This view is obviously popular at the time of writing (oth-erwise the author would not need to address it), so *trendy* is the best meaning. *Flattering* is incorrect since the prevailing view is clearly negative, and *apparent, wholesome,* or *conspicu-ous* do not make sense in context.

8. C

At the end of the first paragraph of Passage 2, the author acknowledges that the scientific ben-efits of manned space missions are debatable. The next paragraph counters this point by argu-ing that manned space flights are the product of an impulse to explore, which should be nurtured, given that it led to the discovery of the Americas, and the third paragraph asserts that such missions would foster beneficial sentiments of curiosity and cooperativeness. The author clearly sees nurturing and inspiring positive sentiments as among the greatest benefits of manned space flight. The other answers are incorrect because they either contradict the argument of the passage (in the case of **A**) or deal with details not considered in the passage (as in the case of **B, D,** and **E**).

9. A

In the final paragraph, the author of Passage 2 introduces the new argument that manned space travel may become essential as life on Earth becomes unbearable, and then makes a case for the idea (dismissed in Passage 1 when the author describes how to "shake off" the effects of the "romantic brew") that the creation of a New Frontier will provide opportunities for social experimentation and hope for enlightened government. **B** is tempting since the author does predict societal and environmental collapse, but this situation is not considered in Passage 1. **D** is also attractive since the author refers to early American history, but the relevant idea about the New Frontier is clearly not shared by the author of the first passage. The author of Passage 2 neither disputes figures offered in Passage 1 (there is none to dispute) nor reconciles his viewpoint with that of its author, so **C** and **E** are incorrect.

10. **E**

The author of Passage 1 argues extensively for the idea that the scientific discoveries of manned space missions are only useful for future manned space missions, and the author of Passage 2, who proposes other benefits, nevertheless does nothing to refute the idea that the scientific advances yielded by manned space experiments are "arguable at best." None of the other answers offers an opinion expressed by either author.

11. **C**

The question asks for a way in which the passages differ in their evaluation of manned space flight, so the right answer must offer a distinction between the two passages that has a bearing on their differing stances regarding sending people into space. **C** is the only answer which meets this requirement—the author of the first passage dismisses the romantic benefits of manned space travel and notes that the scientific benefits can be realized by robotic missions at a lower cost. **A** looks attractive at first since criticism of the romantic nature of support for manned space flight is a major element in the first passage's argument; however, both passages acknowledge that there are romantic motivations behind manned space travel, and the second passage merely differs by understanding this as a good thing rather than a problem. **B** is incorrect because the author of Passage 1 never claims that the scientific findings were falsified, merely that they are only relevant to further manned missions. **D** is incorrect because Columbus is only mentioned in the second passage. **E** is incorrect because only the first passage mentions the impact of space travel on humans, and actually dismisses it as being of use only to future manned space missions.

12. **B**

Both passages focus on arguments concerning the future of manned space flight. Note that both passages draw a distinction between manned and unmanned missions to space. **A** is incorrect because neither passage criticizes the planning of current space missions, though the first passage questions the need for those missions which carry humans into space. **C** and **E** are incorrect because they offer details from the passages, not their shared focus. **D** is incorrect because both passages are focused on one specific aspect of the space program—manned missions, and not the space program in general. This answer is too broad.

PRACTICE SET 3: LONG READING PASSAGE— SOCIAL SCIENCE

<u>Questions 1–10</u> below are based on the following passage.

The following excerpt was taken from an article on the role of the Electoral College in presidential elections.

In 2000, for the first time in 112 years, the candidate who won the popular vote did not become president. This event underscored a curious fact about our political system. Strictly speaking, American voters do not elect their president. A group of people collectively referred to as the Electoral College elects the president on behalf of the
5   American people. How did this strange institution come to be?

Two critical and interlocking concerns shaped how the founders structured the Electoral College. First, the founders wanted to put a check on the popular will. The United States was to be a republic, not a democracy. To the founders, "democracy" meant mob rule. The founders had been horrified by Shays' rebellion in Massachusetts, in
10   which impoverished farmers took up arms against their creditors. By preventing direct popular election of the chief executive, the framers hoped to prevent an American Caesar from destroying the republic by playing on the easily swayed will of the ignorant and unpropertied masses.

Second, the Electoral College was intended to balance the power of large and small
15   states to choose the chief executive. Such a balance had been struck in the legislative branch: the Senate had equal state representation, whereas the House of Representatives featured proportional state representation. Large states had more influence in the House, but all states had equal influence in the Senate. Analogously, the framers empowered state legislatures to appoint or select several electors, the number
20   of which was to equal the sum of that state's representatives and two senators. On a day decreed by Congress, all electors were to meet in their respective states and cast ballots for the presidency. A list recording all votes was to be signed, certified, sealed, and delivered to the president of the Senate (i.e., the vice president of the United States). In a joint session of Congress, the president of the Senate was to unseal and count the
25   votes from all the states. Whichever candidate garnered the most votes became the president-elect, as long as he had a majority of all votes cast. The runner-up became the vice president-elect.

These rules forced the Constitution's framers to take some special cases into account. In the event that two candidates split the Electoral College evenly, both would have a
30   majority, but neither would have the most votes. The election would then go to the House, where each state's delegation would cast a single vote for president. In the event that no candidate carried a majority, the House's state delegations would choose from among the top five vote-getters. In either case, the runner-up in the House election would become vice president. (In the case of a tie for second place, the Senate would vote
35   for one of the two candidates.) The rules by which these contingencies were to be adjudicated demonstrate the founders' desire to balance the power of large and small states. The founders expected that large states would in effect determine who the "candidates" for president were, but small and large states would have an equal say in which candidate ultimately became president.

the
new SAT
Critical
Reading
Workbook

40   For all their concern to account for state loyalty, the founders failed to take party loyalty into account. Political parties arose almost immediately after the Constitution was ratified. Problems with the Electoral College quickly followed. In 1796, John Adams, a Federalist, won the most electoral votes and became president. Thomas Jefferson, a Democratic-Republican, was runner-up to Adams; he became the vice
45 president. Thus, the two top executives were bitter political rivals, an unhappy and unintended state of affairs. In 1804, the Twelfth Amendment stipulated that the Electoral College choose presidents and vice presidents separately.

     A more fundamental structural problem with the Electoral College lay in the founders' anti-democratic intentions. As the nineteenth century progressed, a wave of
50 democratic reform swept Europe and the United States. States began adopting direct popular election of a slate of electors. Political parties began sponsoring their own slate of electors, each of whom pledged to vote for their party's candidate in the Electoral College. The result of each state's popular election began determining which party's slate would take part in the Electoral College.
55   This democratization of the Electoral College had some unintended consequences. First, since presidential elections were still determined state-by-state by winner-take-all electoral votes, rather than by the aggregate popular votes of all states, a candidate could lose the national popular vote and still carry the Electoral College. Second, as party divisions increased and the cost of presidential campaigns skyrocketed,
60 campaigns became increasingly focused on a few contested states, in effect turning a national presidential election into a linked cluster of local elections in which the interests of a few swing states determine national policy decisions. Thus, the Electoral College has failed to fairly balance state interests, as the founders had hoped, while remaining as undemocratic as ever.

1.   The author's primary purpose in the passage is to

   (A) explain the workings of and reasoning behind an institution of the United States government
   (B) encourage protest over the fact that the most popular candidate did not win a recent election
   (C) summarize the history of the founders
   (D) confirm the efficacy of the presidential electoral process
   (E) criticize the founders for their distrust of democracy

2.   In lines 1–2, the author mentions that the 2000 election was the first time in 112 years that the candidate who won the popular vote did not become president because

   (A) the author wants the reader to understand that this was a freak occurrence and thus nothing deserving particular concern
   (B) the author wants to emphasize that elections follow patterns that can be traced over time
   (C) the author wants the reader to understand that this is a problem which has been able to go unnoticed for many years but which now demands our attention
   (D) the author wants the reader to realize that the American political scene in the twenty-first century will resemble that of the nineteenth century more than that of the twentieth century
   (E) the author wants the reader to recognize that elections held at the turn of the century are fundamentally different from those held in the middle of the century

3. In lines 7–8 the author writes, "the United States was to become a republic, not a democracy" to highlight the fact that

   (A) the United States government was intended to approximate the government of Caesar's Roman Empire, not Ancient Greece
   (B) the founders wanted the president to be elected by a select group of people, not the general population
   (C) at the time, the Republican Party was much more powerful than the Democratic Party
   (D) the founders wanted the electoral process to be open to the public
   (E) the founders wanted to make sure that the government did not become a monarchy

4. In lines 10–13, the words "ignorant and unpropertied masses" serve to

   (A) suggest that it was the founders' disdain for poorer and less educated Americans which made them steer away from a truly democratic system for presidential election
   (B) articulate the author's distrust of people who did not go to college and do not own land
   (C) argue for a direct correlation between education and professional success
   (D) assert that, at the time the Electoral College was founded, most Americans were poor and undereducated
   (E) argue that people who do not hold land and are not educated are all alike

5. Which of the following best expresses the point about the legislative branch of the government made in the third paragraph?

   (A) The problems inherent in the legislative branch made it impossible for the Electoral College to offer a fair system.
   (B) The legislative branch served as a model for the Electoral College in the way it attempted to balance the power of large and small states.
   (C) The problems created by the Electoral College would be diffused by the balance of power established by the legislative branch.
   (D) The system in place in the legislative branch made the plan for the Electoral college redundant.
   (E) The system in place in the legislative branch necessitated the proposed organization of the Electoral College.

6. In lines 25–26, the statement that the candidate who received the most votes was elected, "as long as he had a majority of all votes cast," means that

   (A) a candidate would be elected president if he received more votes than anyone else
   (B) a candidate would only be elected president if he received a majority of the popular vote and a majority of the votes from the Electoral College
   (C) a candidate would only be voted president if he received a majority of the votes from the Electoral College and a majority of the votes from the Senate
   (D) a candidate would only be voted president if he received a majority of the votes from the Electoral College and a majority of the votes from the House of Representatives
   (E) if no candidate won more than half the votes, then no candidate would be elected

7. The purpose of the fifth paragraph is to

   (A) undermine the argument made thus far
   (B) convince the reader that the current practice of electing a president and vice president provides the best compromise
   (C) show how a well-intentioned system could lead to unexpected problems
   (D) summarize the points made so far
   (E) give evidence to support an argument offered in the fourth paragraph

8. In line 51, "slate" most nearly means

   (A) rock
   (B) schedule
   (C) tablet
   (D) covering
   (E) list

9. In stating that "as the nineteenth century progressed, a wave of democratic reform swept Europe and the United States" (lines 49–50), the writer assumes that

   (A) the individual states' adoptions of popular elections were part of a broader trend that spanned the Atlantic ocean
   (B) politicians in the United States wanted to be more like their European counterparts
   (C) politicians in Europe wanted to be more like their American counterparts
   (D) women would soon get to vote
   (E) the yearning for democracy that characterized the development of the American government originated in Europe

10. The author's statement in lines 56–58 that "a candidate could lose the national popular vote and still carry the Electoral College" depends on the fact that

   (A) a candidate who wins the popular vote in a certain state by even one vote still receives all of that state's Electoral College votes
   (B) electoral reforms put an end to the practice whereby a president from one party and a vice president from another party could be elected to serve together
   (C) voters in some states would not have their votes counted unless elections in other states resulted in a tie
   (D) incumbent presidents do not need to win a majority of the votes in order to retain office
   (E) the Electoral College is composed of the House of Representatives and the Senate

ANSWERS & EXPLANATIONS

1. **A**

The passage focuses on the way the Electoral College functions and the logic that shaped its design. **B** is tempting because the fact that the most popular candidate did not win the last election seems to be what motivated the author to write the passage, but the passage is focused on explanation rather than protest—it is not until the final sentence that the author expresses dissatisfaction with the electoral system. The passage certainly does not praise the system, however, so **D** is incorrect. **C** and **E** are both incorrect because they offer details that are relevant to the passage but do not accurately represent its main focus.

2. **C**

Even though this question seems to focus on the passage's first sentence, the key to answering it correctly lies in understanding the passage's main idea. Obviously, the author would not have written the passage in the first place if he or she thought the phenomenon did not deserve our concern, so **A** is incorrect. The passage does not examine patterns, ways in which the twenty-first-century political scene will resemble that of the nineteenth century more than that of the twentieth century, or ways in which turn-of-the-century elections differ from mid-century elections, so **B**, **D**, and **E** are all incorrect. The author does seem to think that the potential for the Electoral College to select a candidate other than the one who won the popular vote is worthy of consideration, so **C** is the most logical answer.

PRACTICE SET 3: LONG READING PASSAGE–SOCIAL SCIENCE

ANSWERS & EXPLANATIONS

the
new SAT
Critical
Reading
Workbook

88

3.   C

The second paragraph focuses on the founders' distrust of democracy, or "mob rule" as they thought of it. Instead of a democracy they wanted a republic, in which the president was elected, but only by a small and select group of people. **E** is tempting, since a break with the tradition of monarchy was obviously an important factor in the establishment of the government, but this would have been equally the case if a democracy had been chosen from the beginning. **A** is incorrect because the fear of an American Caesar was uppermost in the founders' minds.

4.   A

The words quoted in the question are more powerfully critical than the rest of the passage, and this alerts the reader to the fact that the author is articulating opinions held by somebody else, specifically the framers of the Electoral College, rather than expressing his or her own opinion (which makes all the other answers incorrect). The author uses such powerful language to suggest that it was the framers' disdainful prejudice against ordinary people's ability to make wise decisions that caused their distrust of democracy in principle, and which motivated them to create an electoral college rather than rely on a popular vote.

5.   B

Lines 17–25 explain that the Electoral College was designed to provide a balance of power between large and small states like that provided by the legislative branch of the government. The other answers are incorrect because they all suggest relationships between the Electoral College and the legislative branch not indicated in the passage.

6.   E

When talking about numbers, the word *majority* is used to refer to a number more than half of the total, so if a majority was required for election, that means that a candidate who received 49% of the votes would not be elected even if his nearest rival won only 45%. **A** is incorrect because it only explains the first half of the statement (that the candidate with the most votes would win). **B**, **C**, and **D** are incorrect because the statement only refers to votes in the Electoral College—the popular vote did not count, and presidential votes were only cast by the House of Representatives, if the Electoral College produced no majority.

7.   C

The first sentence of the fifth paragraph explains that the system the founders created to fairly balance the powers of the states did not anticipate the rise of political parties and the problems that this could cause in cases where the president and vice president were elected from different parties. **B** is tempting because it includes details from the paragraph, but nowhere does the author suggest that the current electoral system represents the best realistic option. **A**, **D**, and **E** do not accurately describe the paragraph.

8.   E

As used in line 62, "slate" is used to refer to the *list* of electors assembled by the political parties. None of the definitions offered by the other answers makes sense in the context of the sentence.

9.   A

The sentence quoted in the question precedes a statement about the states' adoptions of popular elections, implying that what happened in America was part of a trend that also manifested in Europe. There is no suggestion that this trend started on one side of the Atlantic or the other, however, so **B**, **C**, and **E** are all incorrect. No mention is made of women getting the vote, so **D** is incorrect as well.

10.   **A**

The key to answering this question correctly is to go back and read the sentence from which the quoted words were taken. Doing so reveals that a candidate can lose the aggregate, national popular vote but still win the presidency because of the "winner-take-all" nature of the Electoral College. A candidate receives all of a state's electoral votes even if he or she just barely wins that state's popular votes. Since the number of electoral votes is proportional to a state's population, a candidate can lose the national popular vote and yet win the presidency if he or she wins the popular vote by a hair in a few large states with many electoral votes but loses the popular vote by a landslide in many small states with few electoral votes. **B** offers information that is irrelevant to this phenomenon, and from an earlier paragraph. The other answers offer false statements not asserted in the passage.

PRACTICE SET 4: SHORT READING PASSAGE— SCIENCE

Hurricanes are tropical storms with winds of over 75 miles per hour. They begin as thunderstorms that form over areas of the ocean where the water temperature exceeds 81 degrees Fahrenheit. The warmth and moisture in these regions provide the hurricane with its tremendous power, which explains why hurricanes quickly weaken
5 when they pass over cool water and dissipate soon after they hit land.

Although hurricanes themselves are only a real concern to coastal areas, they often give birth to tornadoes. These funnel clouds turn inland, leaving swaths of destruction in their wakes. Tornadoes destroy power lines, damage homes and other property, and are responsible for dozens of deaths every year. These tragedies are becoming less
10 common, however, as new weather technology makes it easier to predict the formation of tornadoes and provide early warning to the areas that may be affected.

1. Using its context in the passage, choose the word that best expresses the meaning of the term "dissipate," found in the final sentence of the first paragraph.

    (A) intensify
    (B) invert
    (C) disappear
    (D) reverse
    (E) deplete

2. What is the main purpose of the second paragraph?

    (A) To convince the reader that hurricanes pose no threat to inland areas
    (B) To explain in more detail the ideas introduced in the first paragraph
    (C) To explain the most dangerous aspect of hurricanes
    (D) To inform the reader why even people who live far from the ocean should be aware of hurricanes
    (E) To assure the reader that the development of new early warning systems will render hurricanes harmless

ANSWERS & EXPLANATIONS

1. **C**

The final sentence of the first paragraph explains that hurricanes draw their power from warmth and moisture, that they weaken in cold weather, and that they *dissipate* over dry land. If they draw their power from warmth and moisture, it seems likely that they would *disappear* over dry land, where moisture is mostly absent, so **C** is the correct answer. **A** is the opposite of the correct answer, and **E** does not make sense in the context of the sentence. **B** and **D** sound more plausible, but the passage does nothing to suggest that hurricanes *reverse* or *invert* over dry land (nor even what it would mean for them to do either of the these things), so **C** remains the best answer.

2. **D**

The second paragraph states that hurricanes themselves only pose a direct threat to coastal areas, but also that they sometimes give rise to tornadoes, which can damage inland areas. Therefore, the paragraph provides a reason why even people who live far from the ocean should be aware of hurricanes—even if the hurricanes themselves won't reach inland, they may produce tornadoes, which very well could. **A** is incorrect because the paragraph only states that hurricanes pose no *direct* threat to inland areas, not that they pose no threat to inland areas at all. **B** is simply inaccurate. **C** is incorrect because the passage does not state or imply that tornadoes are the most dangerous aspect of hurricanes, only the most dangerous to inland areas. **E** is incorrect because the passage does not suggest that early warning systems will render hurricanes harmless, only that they will give people more time to prepare for tornadoes.

PRACTICE SET 5: SHORT READING PASSAGE— SCIENCE

For thousands of years, people believed that owls were more like gods than animals. Even in modern times they have been used to signify wisdom, magic, and power, but the simple truth is that owls are no more divine than other birds. The large, round heads and huge, forward-facing eyes that inclined ancient observers to believe that owls

5   possessed divine intelligence are simply natural adaptations developed to help the predators catch the small animals that make up their food supply.

     Although owls do not possess any of the mystical powers often attributed to them in mythology, they are formidable hunters whose skill surpasses that of other birds of prey. Their acute senses ensure that owls rarely fail to notice a potential meal, and their

10   ability to fly silently means that the unfortunate mouse identified by the owl as its next snack never realizes it is the object of an attack until too late.

1.   In the second sentence of the first paragraph, the word "signify" means

    (A) denote
    (B) magnify
    (C) make important
    (D) insult
    (E) predict

2.   The last sentence of the first paragraph provides

    (A) a summary of the facts presented earlier
    (B) an example to prove a controversial theory presented earlier
    (C) an explanation that rebuts a misconception presented earlier
    (D) an assertion that will be proved later on
    (E) a view that will be contradicted later on

3.   The purpose of the passage as a whole is to

    (A) assure the reader that owls are no different from other birds
    (B) persuade the reader that owls had an important place in ancient mythology
    (C) assert that while owls are not magical they are extraordinary in other ways
    (D) defend an attitude that has recently come under attack
    (E) discredit an idea that has been gaining in popularity

ANSWERS & EXPLANATIONS

1.   **A**

Reading the whole sentence, it is clear that *signify* must mean "stand for" or "represent." The word among the answer choices which has the closest meaning is *denote*. None of the other words in the answer choices comes so close to the apparent meaning of the word in the passage.

2.   **C**

The final sentence of the first paragraph explains that those features of the owl's physiognomy that suggest divine intelligence are really just natural adaptations evolved to help them be more successful hunters. This explanation rebuts the misconception presented at the start of the paragraph that owls are more like gods than humans. None of the other answers offers an accurate description of the sentence.

3.   **C**

The first paragraph deflates the notion that owls are supernatural creatures, but the second half explains that they are exceptionally well-evolved as hunters. **A** is incorrect because the passage makes it clear that owls possess traits not shared with other birds. **B** is incorrect because the passage states the prominence of owls in mythology as a matter of fact, not something of which the reader needs to be persuaded. **D** and **E** are incorrect because the passage does not suggest that any of the ideas or attitudes it covers have become more popular or come under attack. It discredits the idea that owls are magical, but this idea is not shown to be gaining in popularity.

PRACTICE SET 6: SHORT READING PASSAGE— HUMANITIES

One of the features that distinguish traditional Pueblo pottery from other types of clay art is the absence of machinery from all parts of the creative process. The clay is gathered, processed, and finally shaped by hand. Instead of using a potter's wheel to create vases and other round objects, the Pueblo pottery artist rolls clay into long pieces
5 and then painstakingly coils them into layers of circles. Paints are produced from plants and minerals found near the Pueblo village and applied with a handmade brush fashioned from a yucca cactus.

This adherence to tradition is one of the things that make Pueblo pottery so attractive to the art collector. Since the Pueblo potter shuns techniques of mass
10 production, the collector can be sure that every piece of Pueblo clay art is uniquely shaped. This quality also makes examples of Pueblo pottery excellent gifts.

1. According to information provided in the passage, what change to the Pueblo pottery production process would do most to make examples of Pueblo pottery LESS attractive as gifts?

(A) Substitution of synthetic paints for the natural pigments currently used
(B) Changes to the way the clay is gathered and processed
(C) Changes to the type of clay used
(D) The replacement of traditional Pueblo decoration with more modern designs
(E) The introduction of molds to guarantee uniform size and shape

2. The function of the first paragraph is to

(A) establish a thesis that will be refuted in the second paragraph
(B) establish a thesis that will be supported in the second paragraph
(C) provide information that will be used to explain a phenomenon discussed in the second paragraph
(D) present two differing opinions about Pueblo pottery
(E) explain why it is important for people interested in collecting art to learn about Pueblo pottery

3. According to information provided in the passage, what change would do MOST to threaten future production of traditional Pueblo pottery?

(A) The replacement of the traditional process with standardized technology
(B) The increase in popularity of Pueblo pottery
(C) A loss in interest in Pueblo pottery on the part of art collectors
(D) A reduction in the number of Pueblo pottery pieces given as gifts each year
(E) The introduction of new styles of pottery similar to Pueblo pottery

ANSWERS & EXPLANATIONS

PRACTICE SET 6: SHORT READING PASSAGE—HUMANITIES
ANSWERS & EXPLANATIONS

ANSWERS & EXPLANATIONS

1. **E**

The last sentence of the passage asserts that it is the uniqueness of Pueblo pottery pieces that makes them attractive as gifts. If molds were introduced to the production process to guarantee uniform size and shape, this uniqueness would be lost, and pieces of Pueblo pottery would be less attractive as gifts. **A** and **D** are tempting since they propose changes that would seem likely to make Pueblo pottery more "modern" and thus possibly less attractive for gift-giving, but the passage connects the artwork's popularity among gift-givers to the unique shape of each piece.

2. **C**

The first paragraph explains how each piece of Pueblo pottery is shaped and painted by hand. This explains the uniqueness of Pueblo pottery, which is the focus of the second paragraph. None of the other answer choices presents an accurate description of the first paragraph.

3. **A**

Pueblo pottery is defined by its hand-wrought nature. The introduction of standardized technology would threaten the production of *traditional* Pueblo pottery. The changes proposed in **B, C, D**, and **E** might all reduce demand for Pueblo pottery, but this would not necessarily threaten production (there is no suggestion that the primary motivation for production of Pueblo pottery is commercial).

the
new SAT
Critical
Reading
Workbook

96

PRACTICE SET 7: DUAL READING PASSAGE— HUMANITIES

<u>Directions:</u> *The passages below are followed by questions based on the content of the passages and the relationship between the two passages. Answer the questions on the basis of what the passage* <u>states</u> *or* <u>implies</u> *and on any introductory material provided.*

<u>Questions 1–10</u> refer to the following pair of passages.

These passages, adapted from recently published articles, discuss restoring acknowledged masterpieces of art. The first passage is written by a renowned professor of art history. The second is written by a journalist.

Passage 1

Watch reruns of so-called historical dramas on television, and you will have little difficulty in identifying the decade in which the show was originally produced. Does anybody really believe that the long-running 1970s television show *Little House on the Prairie* actually provided an accurate glimpse of nineteenth-century rural life? The actor who played "Pa," for instance, lacked a beard, even though men of that period generally had facial hair. His feathered hair and perfect white teeth further located the
5   show in the 1970s and detracted from the authenticity of the show's intended reconstruction of a bygone era. No one expects the entertainment industry to accurately characterize the past for its own sake; shows like *Little House* use an imagined past to satisfy a nostalgic urge for a way of life that never existed. It is only to be expected that *Little House* says far more about the time in which it was created than the time in which
10   it was set, and one should not get too worked up about it. However, the contemporary trend of restoring classic works of art raises similar issues in a far more serious context.

Restoration, as the word itself implies, assumes that one can recreate an artist's original intent and product. At best, restorers' and museum directors' aesthetic preferences and historical theories drive restorations, for it is impossible to step outside
15   one's historical context. How can restorers be so sure that removing a layer of lacquer isn't merely their subconscious attempt to refashion an artwork according to contemporary tastes? What's "restorative" about that? The "restored" Sistine Chapel may look "authentic" today, but will it still look so when aesthetic and historical theories have changed? Will the newly bright colors heralded as the master's work reborn look as
20   embarrassingly anachronistic as *Little House*? Surely the best approach with any great work of art is to simply leave it alone.

Restorers use the science that informs their task to lend an unwarranted objectivity to their activities. Science's objectivity is beside the point. A scientist can determine the molecular composition of the substances that make up a painting, but a scientist cannot
25   determine the original intent and state of the artist. It will be the art-historian restorer who will use that objective data to decide which substances to remove. The art historian will use his at least partially subjective *judgment*, informed by objective scientific data though it may be, to deem which substances are authentically original. The crux of the problem is that restoration assumes that a contemporary art historian can reproduce
30   the original artwork by recreating the often subconscious decisions of the original artist.

Of course there are occasions in which an artwork must be restored, but only when the work's existence is threatened. But why have so many works of art that are not facing an imminent threat been restored? The reasons, sadly, are more a matter of marketing than conservation. The recent exhortations to clean up Michelangelo's David

35 provide a good example. The Galleria dell'Accademia wanted to spruce David up for his five-hundredth birthday, for they knew that a refurbished David would be catnip for tourists and a windfall for the museum. Not only ticket sales and food concessions but also the inevitable T-shirts, posters, and other cross-marketed products would fill their coffers. Profit, then, and not restoration, is the true cause of the art-restoration craze.

40 Like their Medici forerunners, museum directors' love of art rarely outstrips their love of money.

Passage 2

1 After years of hand-wringing, the verdict followed hard on the heels of the unveiling: Michelangelo's David was once again revealed to be the most beautiful representation of the male form ever sculpted. The art world was greatly relieved. In fact, David had not been restored, but merely cleaned, which had been the museum director's intent. Free

5 from blemishes and stains, that statue again revealed its essential seamlessness. Lines flowed without interruption; shapes melted imperceptibly into one another.

As is usually the case with restorations, controversy had plagued the project, and understandably so. The sad history of poorly restored masterworks has tainted all restorative efforts and prejudiced much of the art world. But the hysteria that

10 surrounded David's restoration was excessive. Chief among the concerns was a debate over the cleaning method. The original restorer wanted to use "dry" techniques to rub off the dirt. When a rival "wet" technique was chosen, he resigned in a huff, convinced that any application of water to the marble would permanently damage the sculpture. His replacement mixed cellulose, clay, and water and wrapped the creamy ointment in rice

15 paper. This compress was then held against the stone, which lifted grime from the surface. This arrangement ensured that only distilled water had any contact with the sculpture.

The recent change in David's appearance was neither the first nor the most intrusive. Far from it: in 1504, an angry mob expressed their political dissent by throwing stones

20 at the statue. David's left arm was broken into three pieces only 23 years later. In the mid-nineteenth century, David was moved from the Piazza della Signoria courtyard, where he had stood exposed to the elements for over 350 years, to his present home, the Galleria dell'Accademia. Well-meaning restorers then gave David an acid bath to remove centuries of accumulated pigeon droppings. In 1991, a deranged tourist

25 attacked David's toe with a hammer. Despite this long history, or perhaps because of it, many scholars are loath to make even the slightest change to David's frame.

It is worth noting, however, that the recent cleaning uncovered a crack on David's left ankle. David's real enemy is not sophisticated, respectful, and painstaking cleaning, but an earthquake—a relatively common event in Italy. Scientists are working now to

30 determine how best to protect David from such an event. In the end, the restoration that so many feared may well have given us the impetus to combat a far more dangerous threat to this great sculpture.

1. In the context of lines 15–17 of Passage 1, the reference to "subconscious attempt" refers to

(A) an actor's inability to portray the time in which he lives
(B) a museum director's questionable motives in organizing a restoration project
(C) a restorer's tendency to favor the aesthetics of his time
(D) an artist's unique ability to recreate the past on canvas
(E) a funder's secret motive in donating to a restoration project

2.   The word "anachronistic" is used in Passage 1, lines 19–20 to signify

    (A) something that is very old
    (B) strong optimism
    (C) something out of place in its time
    (D) peers who share a similar agenda
    (E) color that is bright and flashy in nature

3.   The argument that the desire for profit drives restoration projects in lines 39–41 of Passage 1 would be most STRENGTHENED by which of the following?

    (A) Museum directors have openly stated that profit was the primary motivating
          factor in initiating restoration projects
    (B) No museum restoration project has ever turned a profit
    (C) Many art pieces are difficult to represent on T-shirts and mugs
    (D) Most art restoration projects are undertaken on pieces that are on the verge of
          disintegration, regardless of the popularity of those pieces
    (E) Museums never display restored works of art to the public

4.   According to the author of Passage 2, those who argued that the David should not be cleaned were

    (A) reasonably prudent
    (B) unnecessarily redundant
    (C) overly emotional
    (D) highly biased
    (E) unforgivably ignorant

5.   The word "tainted" in line 8 of Passage 2 most nearly means

    (A) physically putrefied
    (B) morally corrupted
    (C) intrinsically weakened
    (D) inappropriately pigmented
    (E) adversely colored

6.   According to Passage 2, opponents of David's restoration failed to take into account that

    (A) David has been restored without ill effect several times in the past five hundred
          years
    (B) we do not know how Michelangelo would have felt about the restoration
    (C) water might damage the surface of the sculpture
    (D) the current David has withstood many and more severe changes since his original
          creation
    (E) there is a copy of the original David standing in the Piazza della Signoria
          courtyard

7.   Which of the following most accurately describes the organization of the last paragraph of Passage 2?

    (A) The author provides a counterexample that forces him to alter his argument.
    (B) The author relates an unforeseen benefit of an event he has supported.
    (C) The author makes a prediction of future events.
    (D) The author reiterates the argument against his point of view.
    (E) The author supports his position with historical evidence.

8.   Both passages are primarily concerned with

    (A) the successful cleaning of David
    (B) the Sistine Chapel's restoration
    (C) the inadvisability of cleaning paintings with water
    (D) the best way to depict the past on television
    (E) the appropriateness of art restoration

9. The author of Passage 2 would most likely respond to the author of Passage 1's argument that profit drives restorations (lines 39–41) by doing which of the following?

(A) Denying that profit ever motivates restoration projects
(B) Maintaining that it is possible to accurately recreate the original artwork through restoration
(C) Arguing that even if profit motivates restorations, it still ends up preserving and popularizing beautiful and enriching works of art
(D) Insisting that scientific research, not profit, motivates restoration projects
(E) Refuting the notion that art historians can be objective

10. How would the author of Passage 1 most likely respond to the author of Passage 2's report that "the recent cleaning uncovered a crack on David's left ankle" (Passage 2, lines 27–32)?

(A) The restoration caused the crack.
(B) The crack will cut into the museum's projected profits, as visitors will be disappointed.
(C) Since contemporary restorers can't recreate the original intent of the artist whose work they restore, we can't be sure that Michelangelo didn't intend for that crack to be there.
(D) Water caused the crack; the "dry" method should have been used after all.
(E) Further restoration work should begin immediately, as the artwork's existence is threatened.

ANSWERS & EXPLANATIONS

1. C

In lines 17–28 the author discusses his concern that art restorers have a tendency to restore pieces according to the tastes of their time. He uses the Sistine Chapel as an example. The frescoes have been restored and are now very bright, but the author fears that this brightness reflects contemporary taste, and not necessarily the author's original intention. In other words, an art restorer might "subconsciously" be making an "attempt" to restore a piece under the influence of modern tastes.

2. C

To answer this question, first take a look at the sentence in which the word "anachronistic" is used. The author writes: "Will the newly bright colors heralded as the master's work reborn look as embarrassingly anachronistic as *Little House*?" In this part of the passage, the author is making the case that art restorers cannot escape the aesthetic and historical theories of their time. Notice the comparison to reruns of *Little House on the Prairie*. Remember, at the beginning of the passage, the author made the point that even though *Little House* is supposed to take place in the nineteenth century, it has a lot of features of the 1970s. In other words, elements of the show look out of place considering the intended temporal setting, the nineteenth century. *Anachronistic* means exactly this: *ana* means "back" or "backwards"; *chron* means "time." Choice **A** does not quite work. We are looking for a word that specifically addresses things that are erroneously placed in an incorrect temporal setting, not old things. Choice **B** does not fit the tone of the sentence; do the words "suspicion" and "optimism" really go together? You might have been tempted by choice **D** if you thought that the root *chron* in *anachronistic* is related to a "crony," or a peer. But this definition does not fit the context of the sentence. Similarly, you might have been attracted to choice **E** because it mentions "color," but remember, root *chron* means "time." The root *chrom* relates to color, as in "chromatic."

3. A

The author of Passage 1 claims in the final paragraph that profit, not preservation, drives museum directors' initiation of restoration projects. If museum directors came right out and said that profit drives their decision to restore great works of art, that would greatly strengthen the author's argument. Choice **B** may be tempting because it mentions the word *profit*. But it's a distortion—surely, if restoration projects of famous works of art tend not to realize a profit, then their continued occurrence cannot be ascribed to the profit motive! Choice **C** also doesn't strengthen the argument. The author argued that some of the profits of restored artworks comes from reproductions of the newly refurbished image on T-shirts and mugs. If this were difficult to do, for whatever reason, in many cases, that certainly would lower potential profit. Choice **D** actually does not strengthen the author's argument. If it were true that most restoration projects were conducted to prevent the imminent destruction of a piece of art, regardless of its popularity, then profit might not be the primary motivating factor, as the author claims. Finally, if museums never displayed restored artworks, that surely would undermine the author's argument that profit drives restoration projects—it certainly wouldn't *strengthen* that argument. Therefore, **E** is incorrect.

4.　C

In the second paragraph of Passage 2, the author states: "But the hysteria that surrounded David's restoration was excessive." In other words, the author feels that critics were too emotional, or "hysterical." Even if *hysteria* is meant figuratively—and we can't be sure that it isn't meant literally—the conclusion still holds: the author thinks that the critics were far too emotional about the restoration. Furthermore, the original restorer resigned "in a huff," which means, "under the influence of an often-passing burst of self-righteous anger or resentment." Since this is the author's position, he would not agree with choice **A**, as he didn't think the anti-restorationists were being reasonably prudent, or "showing wisdom and good judgment disciplined by reason." Choice **B** is the "left-field" choice—*redundant* means "repetitive." In any ongoing debate, positions will be repeated; this choice distorts that unavoidable fact of debate. Furthermore, the author never mentions redundancy as a fault of the anti-preservationists. You may have been tempted by choice **D** because *biased* is a negative word meaning "unreasonably prejudiced." However, the author's complaint is not about the anti-preservationists' bias, but about the level of emotion with which they pushed their view. One can be biased without being hysterical; one can very calmly state a biased opinion. Choice **E** is also tricky. It's clear that the author thought the anti-preservationists were wrong, but this is far too extreme a description of the author's tone. They weren't *unforgivably* wrong—the entire third paragraph explains why well-meaning people might be reticent about messing around with David after years of abuse. Moreover, there is no evidence that the anti-preservationists were *ignorant*, either. The original restorer, it's safe to infer, was not ignorant; he was merely wrong in this case.

5.　E

The sentence in question is: "The sad history of poorly restored masterworks has tainted all restorative efforts and prejudiced much of the art world." *Tainted* has many meanings—as do most words in vocabulary questions. Which applies here? If you take out *tainted*, the idea is that the history of botched restorations has given restoration a bad name. Which choice matches this? Choices **A**, **B**, and **C**—all legitimate meanings of *tainted*, don't match. Choice **D** is a nasty distractor. The passage is about restoring paintings—and this part of the passage is specifically about how botched restorations have prejudiced much of the art world against restorations. So, you might lunge at **D**, thinking that prior restorers had often used an inappropriate pigment. But you'd have been fooled. Despite the seeming similarity of **D**'s *pigmented* and **E**'s *colored*, the sense of the latter is not literal but figurative. The history of botched restorations has prejudiced many in the art world—has *adversely colored* those people's opinion of all restoration projects.

6. **D**

The author devotes the third paragraph to the violent indignities that David has suffered for half a millennium to show how relatively benevolent and helpful the restoration project was. (What's a gentle cleaning next to stone-throwing or crazed hammering?) Choice **A** is a distortion: we're told of only one restoration—that occurred in the nineteenth century when the statue was bathed in acid. It's unlikely that the author would point to that event as support for his position—in fact, the concluding sentence of the third paragraph acknowledges that the long history of relatively violent assaults on David probably explains some scholars' extreme reticence to cause any further damage, however well-intentioned. **B** is the left-field choice. Nothing is said about what Michelangelo would have thought about the entire issue. **C** is the exact opposite of what you're looking for—the fear of applying water to the sculpture is what made the first restorer walk off the job! And **E** is a distortion. No one cares about a replica of David, no matter where it stands. Everyone was concerned with what to do with the original. Furthermore, according to the passage, the original David was moved from that Piazza della Signoria 150 years ago.

7. **B**

In conclusion, the author notes that despite all the hoopla over David's restoration, the process actually uncovered a far more dangerous threat to the statue: a crack that might cause the statue to crumble during one of Italy's frequent earthquakes. (This is a good example of irony, by the way.) Far from being a counterexample that forces the author to modify his argument, as **A** claims, this unforeseen benefit of David's restoration supports the careful and respectful restoration of great works of art. **C** is incorrect because no actual prediction is made. We're told that scientists are *presently* working on the earthquake problem, which is a potential threat that lies in the *future*. But no specific prediction is made. Even the statement that earthquakes are common in Italy is a historical statement, not a prediction about the future: they've happened in the past; they may happen again in the future. But we can't be sure. The author does not restate counterarguments, as **D** claims, nor does he support his main idea—that the David restoration was a worthwhile undertaking that did not warrant the hysterical reaction of many in the art world—with any historical data. So, **E** is incorrect.

8. **E**

Both passages discuss art restoration, sharing the cleaning of David as a common subject. But while the author of Passage 2 considers the cleaning of David a success, the author of Passage 1, while not commenting on the advisability or success of the venture, uses David's restoration to make a point about how profit, not preservation, motivates restoration projects. Furthermore, the author of Passage 1 mentions David only at the end of the passage; it's not his primary concern. This means that choice **A** cannot be correct. The author of Passage 2 never mentions the Sistine Chapel; this is mentioned only in Passage 1. The author of Passage 2 mentions one restorer's opinion that cleaning *sculptures* with water is inadvisable; the author of Passage 1 does not discuss water as a restorative agent at all. Eliminate choice **C**. The author of Passage 1 mentions television in the first paragraph as an introduction to his discussion about how attainable historical authenticity is, but the author of passage 2 never mentions television at all. The correct choice is **E**, as both authors are chiefly concerned with art restoration.

9. **C**

Items such as these require you to "get inside the head" of the authors. If you were the author of Passage 2, what would you think about the author of Passage 1's argument? Luckily, the SAT usually gives you a distillation of the particular argument (*that profit drives restorations*) and a line reference. Keep in mind tone and the unlikelihood that extreme answers can be correct when checking out the answer choices. **A** seems a bit extreme. Would the author of Passage 2 be so naïve as to deny that profit *ever* plays a role in restoration projects? Unlikely; eliminate. **B** is a distortion. Sure, the author of Passage 1 spends some time arguing that accurate recreation of the original artwork is impossible. But that's not the argument this item is about, nor do we have any evidence of what the author of Passage 2 would think of that argument. **C** seems to be the *most likely* response. The author of Passage 2 spoke of the restored David in glowing, positive terms. His concern about the threat earthquakes may pose to David further reinforces his clear love of the artwork. It's reasonable to infer that this author would feel that the author of Passage 1 is being a bit too purist. One can imagine the author of Passage 2 saying, "If profit motivates the restoration of works like David, then let's hear it for the profit motive! I'm far more concerned with preserving great works of art, no matter where the money comes from." **D** distorts things quite tortuously. The item asks about profit motive—science isn't mentioned. Furthermore, neither author argues that scientific research in and of itself is driving restoration projects. In both passages, science provides tools for the restorers. **E** repeats the distortion of **B**—this item is about profit driving restoration, not about the essential subjectivity of art historians—but with a further twist. The author of Passage 1 argues that art historians *can't* be objective. So the author of Passage 2 can hardly refute something that the author of Passage 1 doesn't maintain at all! Eliminate this choice.

10. **E**

Again, you have to "role-play" here; you're now the author of Passage 1. You've just been told about the crack in David's ankle. How would you *most likely* respond? **A** seems very unlikely. The author of Passage 1 doesn't challenge the efficacy of restoration—he merely doubts that it occurs for reasons of conservation rather than profit. This distractor tries to mix the author of Passage 1 with the anti-restorationists in Passage 2. Always keep your "actors" straight in Reading Passages. Choice **B** superficially refers to the profit-motivation that the author of Passage 1 believes drives restoration projects. But this is hardly a likely reaction to the discovery of the crack itself, and it contains a very shaky inference: that visitors will be so disappointed they won't come to see the famous statue. First, we don't know how big or noticeable the crack is. Second, we don't know that visitors won't rush in even larger droves, worried that David may not be long for this world. Reject the choice. **C** is a distortion. Again, the author of Passage 1 does maintain that contemporary preservationists cannot read the minds of dead artists whose work they restore, but it strains credulity to picture the author of Passage 1, who seems a reasonable, if opinionated person (tone is all-important, remember) seriously maintaining that Michelangelo purposely included an imperfection in his statue! Like **A**, **D** tries to confuse the test-taker by conflating the author of Passage 1, who has nothing to say about "wet" versus "dry" restoration techniques, with the original restorer, who quit when his "dry" technique was rejected. The author of Passage 1's main points were about the impossibility of recapturing original artistic intent and the motivation of profit in restoration projects. Choice **E** is supported by Passage 1: the author states that the only occasion for restorative intervention is in the face of an imminent threat. The potential for an earthquake to destroy an already cracked David would most likely engender this reaction from the author of Passage 1.

PRACTICE SET 8: LONG READING PASSAGE— SCIENCE

The following passage discusses Sir Isaac Newton's three laws of motions.

When we think of the most illustrious physical scientists in history, Newton may be only one of several who come to mind. Aristotle, Pythagoras, Copernicus, Galileo, Kepler, Schrödinger, Einstein, Heisenberg, Planck, Bohr, and Hawking would certainly all be members of this elite club. But if we had to pick a short list, the names would be cut to

5   about two—Newton and Einstein.

Newton's *Principia Mathematica* is generally considered the most important work in the history of physical science. Newton's laws of motion, which he advances in *Principia Mathematica,* describe and predict the actions of all forces and bodies. In this regard, Newton's work dwarfs the greatest discoveries made by virtually any physicist since.

10   Many modern physicists have attained greatness by making findings in extremely specific, often arcane fields of study. But Newton was the first to comprehend such a large chunk of the cosmic plan. What's more, he also developed the complicated mathematical frameworks that prove his theories.

Newton's findings center on three laws, each of which can be summarized in a single

15   statement. Newton's first law states that a body remains at rest, or moves in a straight line at a constant speed, unless acted upon by an outside force. The implications of this law are crucial. All movement is caused by the application of certain forces. Therefore, we can express the movement of a body by the forces that act upon it. Objects don't have energy within themselves. If a ball stops rolling, then some force made it stop—it can't have

20   simply "run out of steam" or lost some sort of internal energy. The ball stops because the force of friction (the floor rubbing against the ball) overtakes the force of the original push a person might have given the ball. The only way to keep the ball moving at the same speed is to continue to push the ball at that speed.

Newton's second law states that the net outside force on an object equals the mass of the

25   object times its acceleration. The greater the force, the more the object accelerates. The larger the mass of an object, the more force is needed to make the object move faster (or move at all, if the object begins at rest). This law is easy to picture: it's easier to throw a baseball than a bowling ball. Also, the harder a ball is thrown, the faster it goes. As intuitive as this may seem to us today, the mathematical implications of the theory are

30   profound. For one, it helpedNewton to determine the exact force of gravity on Earth, which is essential for predicting the motions of all universal bodies (except those of small particles, which are governed by the laws of quantum mechanics).

Newton's third law: "Whenever one body exerts a force on a second body, the second body exerts an equal and opposite force on the first body." More succinctly, for every action

35   there is an equal and opposite reaction. When you push against a wall, the wall exerts an equal force back against your palms. The third law led to a fourth, which is known as Newton's universal law of gravitation: "Two bodies attract each other with a force that is directly proportional to the mass of each body and inversely proportional to the square of the distance between them." This law is perhaps the most important, for it tells us that

40   *everything* in the universe exerts a force on everything else. The sun exerts an attractive gravitational force on the Earth, which keeps us in orbit. But the Earth also exerts an attractive force (though a significantly smaller one) on the sun. You exert a force on the

person sitting next to you, and they exert one back on you.

Newton's laws of motion and his universal law of gravitation allow us to understand
45 and predict virtually every action in our known universe, from the movement of a ball
being hit by a bat to the movement of galaxies. In this sense, Newton's contribution
remains essential to our understanding of the universe. Newton's laws are also the
template Einstein used to develop his theories of relativity, which might be imagined as
extensions of Newton's laws.
50   Now, the goal of many scientists is to formulate an integrative "theory of everything"
that unifies all other theories in physical science. Any theory of everything will be
indebted to Newton's theory—or will evolve out of his theory. His laws describe what we
might call all "practical" events, those that we encounter and observe in everyday life, both
on Earth and beyond. Today, we still rely on Newton's laws in every field of engineering or
55 design, whether it be for making spaceships faster or cars safer, buildings more
structurally sound, or sports equipment more effective. But this kind of summary of the
uses of Newton's laws is only an understatement. They describe our every action, both
those we can see and those that are too small—or too vast—for us to perceive.

1. The primary purpose of this passage is to

    (A) provide a synopsis of Newton's *Principia Mathematica*
    (B) discuss scientists' efforts to formulate a unifying "theory of everything"
    (C) inform the reader of Newton's enduring importance in physical science
    (D) dismiss Newton's accomplishments as outdated
    (E) compare Newton with Einstein

2. The tone of the passage can best be described as

    (A) eulogizing
    (B) pedantic
    (C) informational
    (D) florid
    (E) spare

3. The author states all of the following about Newton EXCEPT:

    (A) Newton's laws allow us to understand the actions of forces and bodies
    (B) Newton's theories influenced Einstein
    (C) Newton developed mathematical frameworks that prove his theories
    (D) Newton developed the theory of relativity
    (E) Newton calculated the exact force of gravity on Earth.

4. The paragraphs that summarize Newton's laws are meant to

    (A) point out flaws in Newton's discoveries
    (B) provide the mathematical proofs behind Newton's discoveries
    (C) explain Newton's discoveries in the context of other scientists' discoveries
    (D) fill in the reader on the fundamentals of Newton's discoveries
    (E) draw broad parallels between the fields of physics and astronomy

5. As it is used in line 11, the word "arcane" most closely means

    (A) obscure
    (B) fascinating
    (C) influential
    (D) technical
    (E) uninteresting

the new SAT Critical Reading Workbook

6. In line 13, what is the meaning of the word "frameworks"?

(A) Branches
(B) Concepts
(C) Outlines
(D) Borders
(E) Instructions

7. Which example does the author use to illustrate Newton's third law?

(A) A person pushing against a wall
(B) A bat hitting a ball
(C) A ball rolling across a surface
(D) The sun's gravitational force keeping the Earth in orbit
(E) Two people sitting next to each other

8. As it appears in line 50, the word "integrative" means

(A) groundbreaking
(B) difficult
(C) superlative
(D) mathematical
(E) uniting

9. The discussion of scientists' efforts toward a "theory of everything" is meant to

(A) demonstrate how much physical science has changed since Newton's time
(B) imply that Newton's discoveries do not compare to current discoveries
(C) dismiss these scientists' efforts as futile
(D) show how Newton's discoveries influence physical science even today
(E) convey how difficult it will be to formulate such a "theory of everything"

10. Which of the following titles best summarizes the passage?

(A) Newton's Laws
(B) Newton and Einstein
(C) Newton's Contributions to Physical Science
(D) Gravity and Relativity
(E) Newton and His Contemporaries

ANSWERS & EXPLANATIONS

1. **C**

The focus of the passage is on Newton, so you can quickly eliminate choice **B**; although the passage does mention the idea of a "theory of everything," such a theory is not the passage's main focus. Although the writer does summarize Newton's laws, no complete summary of *Principia Mathematica* is provided, so eliminate **A**. By no means does the writer dismiss Newton's accomplishments, so eliminate **D**. Finally, in choice **E**, although the writer does link Newton and Einstein in several ways, a comparison of the two scientists is not the focus of the passage. The correct answer is **C**.

2. **C**

C is the only appropriate answer choice. The passage does not mourn Newton's passing, so **A** is inappropriate. **B** does not work because the passage does not dwell on insignificant trivia or details. The prose of the passage is neither excessively flowery, **D**, nor excessively pared down, **E**. Rather, it is meant to provide information, **C**.

the
new SAT
Critical
Reading
Workbook

106

3.   **D**

Throughout the passage, the author explains Newton's achievements and influence. However, it was Einstein rather than Newton who developed the theory of relativity, so answer **D** is correct. Although Einstein drew on Newton's discoveries in developing the theory of relativity, the theory did not arise for several hundred years after Newton's time.

4.   **D**

Eliminate **A** because the author does not attempt to refute Newton's laws. Choice **B** is incorrect because the author does not provide any mathematical background during the course of these paragraphs. Likewise, the author does not provide a broader context of other scientists' discoveries but instead focuses solely on Newton's laws, so **C** is not correct. Finally, eliminate **E** because although the author does mention several astronomical applications of Newton's theories, the passage does not draw broader parallels between the fields of physics and astronomy. The correct answer is **D**—the paragraphs on Newton's laws are meant to convey, in simple form, Newton's fundamental discoveries to readers who might not already be familiar with them.

5.   **A**

You may not know that "arcane" means "mysterious or obscure," but you should be able to figure out its rough meaning from the context of the paragraph. The passage says that many other scientists' great discoveries have been in specific fields that have not had as wide-ranging an impact as Newton's discoveries. From this sentence, you should realize that arcane means something that is not well known or wide-ranging. The best answer is **A**, "obscure."

6.   **B**

"Frameworks" means conceptual structures or ideas, so the best answer is choice **B**, *concepts*. Choices **A** and **D** clearly do not fit into the sentence and can be eliminated. Choice **C**, *outlines*, is too vague and does not fit the meaning of the sentence as well. Choice **E**, *instructions*, implies that Newton drew up instructions for preexisting mathematical concepts when in fact he came up with the concepts himself.

7.   **A**

The author states Newton's third law, paraphrases it, and then gives an example similar to **A**, a person pushing against a wall and the wall exerting a force back on the person's palms. Although the author does use all the other examples to illustrate different aspects of Newton's laws, choice **A** is the only one associated with Newton's third law.

8.   **E**

The author writes that scientists hope to discover a theory "that unifies all other theories in physical science," which implies that "integrative" means "unifying." Choice **E** is the best answer to this question, for "uniting" it is the word with meaning closest to "unifying." Although choices **A**, **B**, and **D** likely are all words that might be used to describe the new theory, they do not fit the context of the sentence as well as **E**, "uniting."

9.   **D**

The author states that "Any theory of everything will be indebted to Newton's theory—or will evolve out of his theory." With this context, it becomes clear that the best answer is **D**, for the author is showing how Newton's discoveries endure in the present day. Choices **B** and **C** are dismissive and can be eliminated immediately. Although **E** is correct in implying that the for-

the new SAT Critical Reading Workbook

mulation of a "theory of everything" will likely be difficult, it is not the main reason that the author includes this discussion in the passage.

10. **C**

Since the focus of this passage is Newton himself, you can eliminate choice **D**. Choice **A** is misleading because the passage does not dwell solely on Newton's laws but also on the broader context of his accomplishments. Likewise, **B** does not work because the passage does not focus exclusively on the relationship between Newton's and Einstein's discoveries. Eliminate **E** because the passage does not discuss Newton's contemporaries—the scientists working along with him at the time—in any depth. The most appropriate answer is **C**, which conveys the fact that the passage is a broad discussion of Newton's enduring contributions to physical science.

the
new SAT
Critical
Reading
Workbook

108

PRACTICE SET 9: LONG READING PASSAGE— FICTION

The following excerpt is taken from a short story about a married couple in Dublin after the husband bites off a small piece of his tongue when he is drunk.

She was an active, practical woman of middle age. Not long before she had celebrated her silver wedding and renewed her intimacy with her husband by waltzing with him to Mr. Power's accompaniment. In her days of courtship, Mr. Kernan had seemed to her a not ungallant figure: and she still hurried to the chapel door whenever a wedding was
5 reported and, seeing the bridal pair, recalled with vivid pleasure how she had passed out of the Star of the Sea Church in Sandymount, leaning on the arm of a jovial well-fed man, who was dressed smartly in a frock-coat and lavender trousers and carried a silk hat gracefully balanced upon his other arm. After three weeks she had found a wife's life irksome and, later on, when she was beginning to find it unbearable, she had
10 become a mother. The part of mother presented to her no insuperable difficulties and for twenty-five years she had kept house shrewdly for her husband. Her two eldest sons were launched. One was in a draper's shop in Glasgow and the other was clerk to a tea-merchant in Belfast. They were good sons, wrote regularly and sometimes sent home money. The other children were still at school.
15 Mr. Kernan sent a letter to his office next day and remained in bed. She made beef-tea for him and scolded him roundly. She accepted his frequent drunkenness as part of the climate, healed him dutifully whenever he was sick and always tried to make him eat a breakfast. There were worse husbands. He had never been violent since the boys had grown up, and she knew that he would walk to the end of Thomas Street and back
20 again to book even a small order.
Two nights after, his friends came to see him. She brought them up to his bedroom, the air of which was impregnated with a personal odor, and gave them chairs at the fire. Mr. Kernan's tongue, the occasional stinging pain of which had made him somewhat irritable during the day, became more polite. He sat propped up in the bed by pillows
25 and the little color in his puffy cheeks made them resemble warm cinders. He apologized to his guests for the disorder of the room, but at the same time looked at them a little proudly, with a veteran's pride.
He was quite unconscious that he was the victim of a plot which his friends, Mr. Cunningham, Mr. M'Coy and Mr. Power had disclosed to Mrs. Kernan in the parlor. The
30 idea had been Mr. Power's, but its development was entrusted to Mr. Cunningham. Mr. Kernan came of Protestant stock and, though he had been converted to the Catholic faith at the time of his marriage, he had not been in the pale of the Church for twenty years. He was fond, moreover, of giving side-thrusts at Catholicism.
When the plot had been disclosed to her, Mrs. Kernan had said:
35 "I leave it all in your hands, Mr. Cunningham. "
After a quarter of a century of married life, she had very few illusions left. Religion for her was a habit, and she suspected that a man of her husband's age would not change greatly before death. She was tempted to see a curious appropriateness in his accident and, but that she did not wish to seem bloody-minded, would have told the
40 gentlemen that Mr. Kernan'stongue would not suffer by being shortened. However,

109

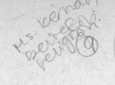

Mr. Cunningham was a capable man; and religion was religion. The scheme might do good and, at least, it could do no harm. Her beliefs were not extravagant. She believed steadily in the Sacred Heart as the most generally useful of all Catholic devotions and approved of the sacraments. Her faith was bounded by her kitchen, but, if she was put

45 to it, she could believe also in the banshee and in the Holy Ghost.

1. It can be inferred that Mrs. Kernan "still hurried to the chapel door whenever a wedding was reported" (lines 4–5) because

   (A) she knows people who are attending the weddings
   (B) the weddings remind her of her own wedding, which she remembers fondly
   (C) she yearns for romance, which her marriage to Mr. Kernan lacks
   (D) watching weddings helps her overcome her boredom now that her sons are grown
   (E) she is curious to see what the bride is wearing

2. In relation to the first paragraph, the first sentence of the second paragraph (line 15) serves to

   (A) move away from the character description of the first paragraph and advance the action of the story
   (B) build on the description in the first paragraph of Mrs. Kernan's sons
   (C) enhance the reader's understanding of Mrs. Kernan's character
   (D) offer a description of Mrs. Kernan that contrasts with the description given in the first paragraph
   (E) provide a specific example of the generalizations made in the first paragraph

3. The second paragraph suggests that the Kernans' marriage is characterized primarily by

   (A) Mr. Kernan's violence against his wife
   (B) Mrs. Kernan's patience with her husband
   (C) Mr. Kernan's fondness for his wife's beef-tea
   (D) Mrs. Kernan's irritation with her husband's frequent drunkenness
   (E) Mr. Kernan's willingness to go to the store for his wife

4. Which of the following best captures the meaning of the word "impregnated" in line 22?

   (A) marked by
   (B) fertilized
   (C) saturated
   (D) replaced
   (E) oppressed

5. The reference to Mr. Kernan's tongue in lines 23–24 is used to describe both his actual tongue and

   (A) the kind of language he uses
   (B) his physical appearance
   (C) the gestures he makes
   (D) warm cinders
   (E) his personal odor

6. The word "stock" in line 31 most nearly means

   (A) birth
   (B) structure
   (C) framework
   (D) faith
   (E) lineage

7. In the passage, Mr. Kernan is characterized as

(A) foolish and excessive
(B) sensible and intelligent
(C) stubborn and unreasonable
(D) proud of his accomplishments
(E) irreverent but generally considerate

8. It can be inferred from the fourth paragraph (lines 28–33) that the goal of the friends' plot is to

(A) turn Mr. Kernan into a better husband
(B) cure Mr. Kernan of his alcohol abuse
(C) make Mr. Kernan a good, practicing Catholic
(D) go to Thomas Street for Mrs. Kernan while her husband recovers
(E) donate money and furniture to the Kernans

9. The last paragraph suggests that Mrs. Kernan's belief in religion is

(A) practical but faithful
(B) fervently pious
(C) nonexistent
(D) superficial
(E) marked by skepticism

10. Throughout the passage, the primary focus is on

(A) Mr. Kernan's recovery
(B) the relationship between Mr. Kernan and his friends
(C) the practice of Catholicism
(D) Mrs. Kernan's attitudes toward her marriage and religion
(E) the plot hatched against Mr. Kernan

ANSWERS & EXPLANATIONS

1. **B**

The key to answering this question is to read past the quoted material. The sentence says, "she still hurried to the chapel door whenever a wedding was reported and, seeing the bridal pair, recalled with vivid pleasure how she had passed out of the Star of Sea Church in Sandymount, leaning on the arm of a jovial well-fed man, who was dressed smartly in a frock-coat and lavender trousers and carried a silk hat gracefully balanced upon his other arm." The second part of the sentence describes Mrs. Kernan's memory of her own wedding, and it says that she recalls her wedding "with vivid pleasure." This sentence suggests that nostalgia for her own wedding is one of the reasons why Mrs. Kernan watches other people's weddings, so the best answer to this question is **B**. You can also arrive at this answer through elimination. The passage does not say that Mrs. Kernan knows people at the wedding, so you can rule out **A**. It never implies that she yearns for romance, so you can rule out choice **C**. Finally, the passage does not talk about her boredom or her curiosity, so you can rule out **D** and **E**.

2. **A**

The first paragraph focuses on giving a character description of Mrs. Kernan. The second paragraph begins with the sentence, "Mr. Kernan sent a letter to his office next day and remained in bed." This sentence represents a shift away from the character description of the first paragraph, and it describes an action in the plot. The best answer to this question is **A**.

3. **B**

This question asks you to make a general characterization based on the description given in the second paragraph of the Kernans' relationship. While the paragraph does mention violence, the narrator notes that Mr. Kernan "had never been violent since the boys had grown up," so choice **A** is wrong. You can rule out choice **C** because the passage never implies that Mr. Kernan likes the beef-tea that his wife makes for him, and you can rule out choice **D** since the passage never says that Mrs. Kernan was irritated by her husband's drunkenness. While choice **E** seems to be a true statement (the paragraph says that "he would walk to the end of Thomas Street and back again to book even a small order"), his willingness to go there doesn't adequately characterize their relationship. The best answer is choice **B**. The third sentence indicates that **B** is the right answer: "She accepted his frequent drunkenness as part of the climate, healed him dutifully whenever he was sick and always tried to make him eat a breakfast." Words like "accepted" and "dutifully" suggest Mrs. Kernan's patient resignation to her life and duties.

4.   **C**

In the context of this sentence, the word "impregnated" means "filled or saturated," so the correct answer to this question is choice **C**. If you can't identify the answer, you can improve your chances of guessing correctly by first eliminating obviously wrong answers. The best method of elimination is to substitute the answer choices into the sentence for "impregnated." If you use this method, you should see that *fertilized*, *replaced*, and *oppressed* don't make sense in the context of the sentence, so you can rule out choices **B**, **D**, and **E**.

5.   **A**

In the sentence "Mr. Kernan's tongue, the occasional stinging pain of which had made him somewhat irritable during the day, became more polite," the tongue describes both the actual organ in Mr. Kernan's mouth and the language he uses. The correct answer to this question is **A**.

6.   **E**

As its used in this passage, "stock" means "lineage" or "family," so the correct answer is **E**. If you don't know the definition of "stock," you can narrow down the answer choices through elimination. Since neither *framework* or *structure* makes sense in the context of the sentence, you can rule out choices **B** and **C**, leaving you with a one in three chance of guessing the correct answer.

7.   **E**

Nothing in the passage suggests that Mr. Kernan has any of the characteristics given in choices **A**, **B**, or **C**, so you can rule out those answer choices. Although Mr. Kernan appears to be proud of his injury at the end of the third paragraph, the passage does not suggest that he is proud in general of his accomplishments. The correct answer is choice **E**. The narrator of the passage describes Mr. Kernan's verbal lack of respect for Catholicism, and Mrs. Kernan thinks that her husband's "tongue would not suffer by being shortened" (in other words, he talks too quickly and too rashly), so you can characterize him as "irreverent," or "lacking proper respect or seriousness." The passage also implies that Mr. Kernan is " considerate" when it describes his willingness to run errands for his wife.

8.   **C**

The fourth paragraph begins by saying that Mr. Kernan is the victim of his friends' plot. Since the rest of the paragraph is devoted primarily to Mr. Kernan's religious background and his attitude toward Catholicism, you can reasonably infer that the friends' plot has to do with religion, so **C** seems like a likely answer. You can confirm that **C** is the right answer by eliminating the other answer choices. Since the passage never mentions making Mr. Kernan a better husband, you can rule out choice **A**. There is no mention of Mr. Kernan's drinking after the second paragraph, so you can also rule out choice **B**. Choice **D** tries to lure you off track by mentioning

Thomas Street, an unrelated but specific piece of information from the passage. There is no mention of donating money or furniture to the Kernans, so you can eliminate choice **E**.

9. **A**

Since the last paragraph describes Mrs. Kernan's belief in religion, you can immediately eliminate choice **C**, which says that her belief in religion does not exist. The sentence "Her beliefs were not extravagant" should help you eliminate choice **B**, which says that Mrs. Kernan is *fervently pious,* or "intensely religious and devoted to worship." The paragraph never says or implies that Mrs. Kernan is superficial in her religious belief or skeptical of Catholicism, so you can rule out choices **D** and **E**. Choice **A** is the best answer because the paragraph describes her as faithful ("if she was put to it, she could believe also in the banshee and the Holy Ghost") and practical ("Her beliefs were not extravagant").

10. **D**

The main focus of this passage is Mrs. Kernan. Even though the passage contains a couple of paragraphs that describe Mr. Kernan, the narrator tends to describe him from the point of view of his wife. Since the passage opens with a discussion of Mrs. Kernan's views about marriage and ends with a discussion of her views about religion, the best answer to this question is **D**.

PRACTICE SET 10: DUAL READING PASSAGE— HISTORY

The following passages discuss the reign of the nineteenth-century British monarch Queen Victoria after the death of her husband, Prince Albert, to whom she was devoted. Passage 1 is a biographical account of the Queen's mourning period written in the late twentieth century. Passage 2 is a biographical account of the mourning period written in the early twentieth century.

Passage 1

Perhaps the most significant turning point in Queen Victoria's life was the death of her husband, Prince Albert, in December 1861. His death sent Victoria into a deep depression, and she stayed in seclusion for many years, rarely appearing in public. She mourned him by wearing black for the remaining forty years of her life.

5   Albert's death came suddenly. In November 1861, he contracted typhoid fever. He lay sick in bed for several weeks, finally succumbing to the disease on December 14. He was only forty-two years old. Victoria was devastated. She wrote to her daughter Victoria shortly afterwards: "How I, who leant on him for all and everything—without whom I did nothing, moved not a finger, arranged not a print or photograph, didn't put

10   on a gown or bonnet if he didn't approve it shall go on, to live, to move, to help myself in difficult moments?"

    The Queen turned mourning into the chief concern of her existence the next several years. The Prince's rooms in their residences were maintained exactly as he had them when he was alive. Her servants were instructed to bring hot water into his dressing

15   room every day as they had formerly done for his morning shave. She had statues made of him, displayed mementos of his around the royal palaces, and spent most of her time secluded in Windsor Castle or in Balmoral up in Scotland, where she had formerly spent so many happy times with her husband.

    After the first year, her mourning came to be viewed by many in Britain as

20   obsessive, and public unease arose about the Queen's state of mind and the state of the monarchy generally. This unease was aggravated by Victoria's refusal to appear in public except on the rarest occasions. She made her first public appearance only on October 13, 1863, and then only to unveil a statue of Albert at Aberdeen, Scotland. She appeared publicly in London on June 21, 1864, riding out through the streets in an

25   open carriage. She did not personally appear to open Parliament until the 1866 session, and then only reluctantly.

    During Victoria's years of mourning and seclusion she reformed the British Army. By 1870, Victoria abolished the Army's patronage system, which had allowed offices to be purchased and granted as gifts. The Army Regulation Bill, which was designed to

30   bring about reforms, was rejected in the House of Lords in 1870, and the changes only came about by royal warrant from the Queen. Victoria approved of restricting royal power in the military, as the reform included the subordination of the role of Commander-in-Chief—a royal appointee, Victoria's cousin, the Duke of Cambridge—to below that of the Secretary of State. She was reluctant to go ahead with these reforms,

35   but judged it the right thing to do despite her personal inclinations to support royal patronage.

Passage 2

1   The death of the her husband Albert, the Prince Consort, was the central turning-
point in the history of Queen Victoria. She herself felt that her true life had ceased
with her husband's, and that the remainder of her days upon earth was of a twilight
nature—an epilogue to a drama that was done.

5   With appalling suddenness Victoria had exchanged the serene radiance of
happiness for the utter darkness of woe. In the first dreadful moments those about her
had feared that she might lose her reason, but the iron strain within her held firm, and
in the intervals between the intense paroxysms of grief it was observed that the Queen
was calm. She remembered, too, that Albert had always disapproved of exaggerated
10   manifestations of feeling, and her one remaining desire was to do nothing but what he
would have wished.

Yet there were moments when her royal anguish would brook no restraints. One day
she sent for the Duchess of Sutherland, and, leading her to the Prince's room, fell
prostrate before his clothes in a flood of weeping, while she adjured the Duchess to tell
15   her whether the beauty of Albert's character had ever been surpassed. At other times a
feeling akin to indignation swept over her. "The poor fatherless baby of eight months,"
she wrote to the King of the Belgians, "is now the utterly heartbroken and crushed
widow of forty-two! My LIFE as a HAPPY one is ENDED! The world is gone for ME! . .
. Oh! to be cut off in the prime of life—to see our pure, happy, quiet, domestic life, which
20   ALONE enabled me to bear my MUCH disliked position, CUT OFF at forty-two—when
I HAD hoped with such instinctive certainty that God never WOULD part us, and
would let us grow old together (though HE always talked of the shortness of life)—is
TOO AWFUL, too cruel!" The tone of outraged Majesty seems to be discernible. Did she
wonder in her heart of hearts how the Deity could have dared?

25   Though the violence of her perturbations gradually subsided, her cheerfulness did
not return. For months, for years, she continued in settled gloom. Her life became one
of almost complete seclusion. Arrayed in thickest crepe, she passed dolefully from
Windsor to Osborne, from Osborne to Balmoral. Rarely visiting the capital, refusing to
take any part in the ceremonies of state, shutting herself off from the slightest
30   intercourse with society, she became almost as unknown to her subjects as some
potentate of the East. They might murmur, but they did not understand. What had she
to do with empty shows and vain enjoyments? No! She was absorbed by very different
preoccupations. She was the devoted guardian of a sacred trust. Her place was in the
inmost shrine of the house of mourning. That, and that only was her glorious, her
35   terrible duty. For terrible indeed it was. As the years passed her depression seemed to
deepen and her loneliness to grow more intense. "I am on a dreary sad pinnacle of
solitary grandeur," she said. Again and again she felt that she could bear her situation
no longer—that she would sink under the strain.

1.   The quotation in lines 8–11 suggests that Victoria mourned her husband's death primarily
     because

     (A) he had managed all of her affairs
     (B) he had played an integral part in every aspect of her life
     (C) she would not be able to have more children
     (D) he had died at an unexpectedly young age
     (E) he could no longer advise her on political matters

2.   According to Passage 1, Victoria did all of the following to mourn her husband EXCEPT

     (A) keep everything as it had been before his death
     (B) display his mementos around her palaces
     (C) erect statues of him
     (D) appear publicly to open Parliament
     (E) wear black for the remainder of her life

the
new SAT
Critical
Reading
Workbook

115

3. The tone of Passage 1 can best be described as

   (A) informal
   (B) comic
   (C) academic
   (D) passionate
   (E) satirical

4. Which of the following titles best summarizes Passage 1?

   (A) The Power of the Prince Consort: Prince Albert's Influence on Queen Victoria
   (B) The Fruitful Marriage of Queen Victoria and Prince Albert
   (C) Queen Victoria and the Victorians
   (D) The Legacy of Queen Victoria
   (E) The Reign of Queen Victoria during her Mourning Period

5. The comparisons of Victoria's mourning to twilight and to an epilogue in lines 2–4 of Passage 2 serve to

   (A) illustrate how Victoria considered her life to be a stage drama
   (B) indicate that the most prominent period of Victoria's reign was her mourning period
   (C) underscore Victoria's feeling that the main part of her life was her marriage to Albert
   (D) describe how Victoria's mourning took place mostly in the evenings
   (E) detract from the seriousness and intensity of her feelings after Albert died

6. The sentence "No!" in line 32 of Passage 2 represents

   (A) the author's objection to the statement
   (B) the reader's response to the passage
   (C) a meaningless interjection
   (D) the imagined response of Victoria
   (E) the public's outcry against the mourning period

7. In line 12 of Passage 2, "brook" most nearly means

   (A) tolerate
   (B) stream
   (C) punish
   (D) advocate
   (E) refuse

8. The word "adjured" is used in line 14 to mean

   (A) forbade
   (B) allowed
   (C) asked
   (D) commanded
   (E) reprimanded

9. With which of the following statements would the authors of the passages most likely agree?

   (A) Victoria's obsessive mourning harmed the state of the country.
   (B) Albert was not worthy of such diligent mourning from his wife.
   (C) The public was wrong to criticize Victoria for her long mourning period.
   (D) Victoria accomplished a great deal of political reform during her mourning period.
   (E) Albert's death was the most catastrophic event in Victoria's life.

10. The main difference between the two descriptions of Victoria's mourning period is that

(A) Passage 1 focuses on the political implications of the mourning period, while Passage 2 focuses on its social implications
(B) Passage 1 puts more emphasis on Victoria's actions during her mourning period than Passage 2 does
(C) Passage 1 is more interested in Victoria's emotional reaction to Albert's death than Passage 2 is
(D) Passage 1 praises Victoria's behavior, while Passage 2 condemns her behavior
(E) Passage 1 is less interested in giving a factual account of the mourning period than Passage 2 is

ANSWERS & EXPLANATIONS

1. B

When answering this question, you should reread the quotation to which the question refers: "How I, who leant on him for all and everything—without whom I did nothing, moved not a finger, arranged not a print or photograph, didn't put on a gown or bonnet if he didn't approve it shall go on, to live, to move, to help myself in difficult moments?" Victoria says that she relied on Albert "for all and everything;" in other words, he played an important role in every aspect of her life. Her chief cause for grief, according to this quotation, is that she has lost someone integral to her life, so choice **B** is the best answer to this question.

2. D

This question asks you to figure out what Victoria did NOT do to mourn her husband, so make sure you don't identify something that she did do. If you go back to the passage, particularly to the third paragraph, you will see that Victoria did all of the answer choices but appear publicly to open Parliament. The author states in the fourth paragraph that Victoria "did not personally appear to open Parliament until the 1866 session, and then only reluctantly." Although Victoria did eventually open Parliament, this gesture was not part of her mourning for Albert, so choice **D** is the correct answer to this question.

3. C

Passage 1 is a pretty neutral examination of Victoria's mourning period, so the best answer to this question is choice **C**. If you feel uncertain about this answer, you can try eliminating the other answer choices first. The passage is neither informal nor comic nor satirical, although these descriptions could apply to Passage 2, so you can rule out choices **A**, **B**, and **E**. The author of Passage 1 never betrays any extreme emotion, so you can rule out choice **D**, thus leaving you with the correct answer, **C**.

4. E

In order to answer this question, try to identify the main focus of this passage. The passage describes Victoria's reign after the death of her husband, so the best title for the passage is choice **E**. You can confirm this answer by eliminating the other answer choices. Choice **A** puts too much emphasis on Prince Albert. Choice **B** focuses on the period of Victoria and Albert's marriage, although the passage never actually describes what their marriage was like. Choice **C** focuses on Victoria and the Victorians, but the Victorian public is mentioned only once in the passage. Choice **D** describes Victoria's legacy, but the passage focuses on Victoria's life, not on what Victoria left to future generations.

5. **C**

The author compares Victoria's mourning period to the twilight of the day and the epilogue of a drama. The twilight is the end of the day, and the epilogue is what comes after a drama, or play, is finished. These comparisons emphasize that Victoria's life with Albert represented the main part of her life, or her "true life," so choice **C** is the best answer to this question. You can rule out the other answer choices to double-check this answer. The passage never implies that Victoria thought her life was a stage drama, so choice **A** is wrong. Since twilight is dwarfed by the day and since an epilogue is dwarfed by a play, choice **B** is wrong, because it says that the mourning period is the most prominent part of Victoria's life. Choice **D** incorrectly takes the comparison too literally, and finally, there is no evidence for choice **E** in the passage.

6. **D**

If you refer back to the passage, you can immediately rule out choices **B** and **E** because neither the reader nor the public is mentioned in this part of the passage. You can also rule out choice **C** since the interjection is not meaningless. In order to answer the question, you need to decide whether the interjection "No!" represents the author's or Victoria's response. Although the author does not make it explicit, in this part of the passage he is trying to portray Victoria's thoughts as she would have thought them. Thoughts such as "she was the devoted guardian of a sacred trust" do not necessarily represent the author's view, but they do represent Victoria's view of herself. The interjection "No!" is how the author imagines Victoria would respond to the implication that she is affected by "empty shows and vain enjoyments," so choice **D** is the best answer to this question.

7. **A**

As it is used in this context, "brook" means "tolerate," so choice **A** is the correct answer. If you don't know the meaning of brook, you can answer this question through elimination. You can immediately rule out choice **B** because it does not make sense in the context of the sentence: "stream" is a noun, while you're looking for a verb. You can substitute the remaining answer choices into the sentence for "brook" to see whether they make sense. Since the paragraph describes how Victoria brooked her restraint and showed much emotion, you can infer that "brook" has a positive meaning, and you can rule out words with negative meanings, such as choices **C** and **E**. By eliminating these answer choices, you increase your chances of guessing correctly to one in two.

8. **D**

The definition of "abjured" is "commanded," so the correct answer to this question is **D**. If you don't know this definition, try eliminating the other answer choices to improve your odds of guessing correctly. The best way to eliminate is to substitute the other answer choices into the original sentence and see which ones do not make sense in context. Neither choice **A** nor choice **E** makes sense in the context of the sentence, so you can rule them out. Choice **B** seems unlikely because you can infer from the passage that Victoria instigates most of the conversations praising her husband. Although both choices **C** and **D** make sense in the context of the sentence, **D** is a more likely answer because in her position as queen, Victoria would most likely command her subjects to do something than simply ask them to do something.

9. **E**

This question asks you to identify a point on which the authors of the two passages would agree. If you read the first sentences of each passage, you will see that both authors consider the death of Albert to be the main "turning point" in Victoria's life, and each passage goes on to describe Victoria's depression after her husband's death. Based on this, you can infer that both author's consider her husband's death to be the most catastrophic event in her life, so choice **E** is the best answer to this question. You can also answer this question by ruling out the other answer choices. Neither of the authors implies that Victoria's mourning harmed her country, and neither of the passages implies that Albert was unworthy of her mourning, so choices **A** and **B** are wrong. Although the passages mention that the public grew tired of Victoria's mourning, neither one explicitly criticizes her on this point, so you can rule out choice **C**. Only Passage 1 mentions a piece of political reform passed during the mourning period; Passage 2 focuses exclusively on Victoria's feelings, so choice **D** is wrong.

10. **B**

While the passages are very similar, there is a subtle difference in approach to the subject matter. Passage 1, which is more academic in tone than Passage 2, focuses slightly more than Passage 2 on Victoria's actions during her mourning period. For example, it discusses Victoria's efforts to keep the memory of her husband alive; it describes how she withdrew from the public eye; and it describes a piece of reform that she passed during this period. The second passage, by contrast, focuses on Victoria's emotional state after her husband's death. Thus choice **B** is the best answer to this question.

the new SAT
Critical
Reading
Workbook

PRACTICE SET 11: LONG READING PASSAGE— LITERARY CRITICISM

The following passage was written by a literary critic about the use of shoes in Flannery O'Connor's short stories and novels.

Despite the growing mass of criticism on Flannery O'Connor, a single recurring detail in her fiction has either escaped the notice of most critics or been deemed unworthy of their attention: the shoe. But in her work, O'Connor draws the reader's attention to shoes so often that they should not be ignored. With the exception of

5 "Greenleaf" and "The Comforts of Home," all of O'Connor's fiction contains shoe imagery, and shoes assume meanings beyond their pedestrian function. In fact, O'Connor's characters are often inseparable from the shoes they wear.

In O'Connor's fiction, shoes are a means of identifying social class and signaling the personalities of her characters. In "Revelation," the protagonist, Mrs. Turpin, looks

10 around the waiting room in her doctor's office and classifies its occupants by the types of shoes they wear. A well-dressed lady wears red and gray suede shoes that match her dress; an ugly, bookish girl wears thick Girl Scout shoes (a type of shoe that appears often in O'Connor's writing); a trashy woman wears flimsy bedroom slippers made of black straw threaded with gold braids. Mrs. Turpin herself wears "her good black

15 patent leather pumps," a sign of respectability. This method of classification occurs again in "Everything that Rises Must Converge." In this story, riders on a bus are identified primarily by their shoes. One of the women on the bus is given no name or description other than "the owner of the red and white canvas sandals." O'Connor further develops the notion that the shoe is connected to a person's identity in

20 *Wise Blood*. In this novel, Enoch buries all of his clothes before donning an ape suit and relinquishing his human identity. He then discovers that he is still wearing his shoes. To complete his transformation into an animal, he removes his shoes and flings them aside.

Other characters in O'Connor's stories have a harder time discarding their identities

25 than Enoch does. In "A Late Encounter with the Enemy," Sally Poker Sash remembers attending the premiere of *Gone with the Wind* in Atlanta with her grandfather, a very old and cantankerous man and a former Confederate general. The prestige of attending the event swells Sally's sense of self-importance, but her pride is dashed when, standing on the stage next to her grandfather, she realizes that she is wearing her old

30 pair of brown Girl Scout Oxfords underneath her evening gown instead of the silver slippers she planned to wear. Despite Sally's efforts to remake her appearance for the evening, her unsophisticated, clumsy shoes betray her true self.

Sally's shoes also warn the reader about the precarious perch upon which pride and vanity are built. Sally's realization that she is wearing the brown shoes recalls the

35 traditional literary metaphor of the peacock. Clergymen used the peacock to represent the folly of pride, vanity, and materialism. The first notable use of the peacock metaphor occurred in the fourteenth century in *Piers Plowman*. In this poem, the peacock represents vanity. The bird proudly displays its magnificent tail, but when it looks down and notices its ugly feet, it becomes crestfallen: a reminder that vanity is a weakness.

40 The peacock's feet are analogous to Sally's shoes. Despite the grand occasion and her beautiful dress, Sally lets vanity get the better of her and destroy her evening.

Sally's vanity has more dire consequences later in the story. At her graduation
ceremony from teacher's college, she wants to show off by having her grandfather
appear on stage with her. By having him participate in the graduation ceremony, she
45 hopes to show everyone that she has descended from an important family and thus that
she is someone far above average. The stress and the heat of the day prove too much for
the old man, and when he is pushed on stage in his wheel chair, Sally Poker Sash sees
that he has died in order to serve her vanity.

1. The primary purpose of this passage is to

(A) explain why critics should examine the use of shoe imagery in O'Connor's writings
(B) summarize the use of shoe imagery in "A Late Encounter with the Enemy" and
    "Everything that Rises Must Converge"
(C) list and describe the most important mentions of shoes in O'Connor's short stories
    and novels
(D) praise O'Connor for her subtle use of shoe imagery and the peacock metaphor
(E) examine some of the ways in which O'Connor uses shoe imagery in her writing

2. The author's attitude toward critics who fail to recognize the importance of shoes in
    O'Connor's work can best be described as one of

(A) surprised pleasure
(B) mild annoyance
(C) strong disagreement
(D) disbelief
(E) unbridled anger

3. According to the second paragraph, what does Mrs. Turpin notice in "Revelation"?

(A) The shoes worn by people in the doctor's waiting room
(B) The occupations of people in the doctor's waiting room
(C) The clothing worn by people in the doctor's waiting room
(D) The shoes worn by people on the bus
(E) The clothing worn by people on the bus

4. Which of the following does the author give as a difference between Enoch and Sally Poker
    Sash?

(A) Enoch does not experience the same kind of disappointment that Sally does.
(B) Enoch is able to shed his identity, while Sally is not.
(C) Enoch treats his grandfather poorly, while Sally does not.
(D) Enoch does not want to impress other people, while Sally does.
(E) Enoch wants to be an animal, while Sally wants to be a beautiful woman.

5. Which of the following statements best describes the way in which the third paragraph in the
    passage is related to the second?

(A) The third paragraph refutes the claims made in the second paragraph.
(B) The third paragraph makes a generalization based on the statements in the
    second paragraph.
(C) The third paragraph extends the arguments made in the second paragraph to
    their logical limit.
(D) The third paragraph adds further evidence to the argument made in the second
    paragraph.
(E) The third paragraph is not related to the second paragraph.

6. What do lines 29–32 suggest about the nature of people who wear Girl Scout shoes?

(A) They are old and worn.
(B) They are unsophisticated.
(C) They are not interested in dressing up.
(D) They are smart and practical.
(E) They are ugly and bookish.

7.   According to the passage, the peacock in *Piers Plowman* represents

(A) shoes
(B) human feet
(C) beauty
(D) sorrow
(E) vanity

8.   According to the passage, Sally Poker Sash is a character in

(A) "Greenleaf"
(B) "The Comforts of Home"
(C) "A Late Encounter with the Enemy"
(D) "Revelation"
(E) *Wise Blood*

9.   Which of the following best captures the meaning of "analogous to" as used in line 40?

(A) different from
(B) the opposite of
(C) unrelated to
(D) similar to
(E) the same as

10. What does the author's description of Sally Poker Sash imply about Sally's relationship with her grandfather?

(A) He dotes on her and always gives in to her demands.
(B) He blames her for the embarrassing moments they have on stage.
(C) She is ashamed of him and does not speak to him.
(D) She is proud of his accomplishments and takes care of him.
(E) She treats him like a trophy and uses him to show off.

ANSWERS & EXPLANATIONS

1.   **E**

The author's main purpose in writing the passage is to examine ways in which O'Connor uses shoe imagery in her writings, so the correct answer is **E**. Although the author states that critics rarely address shoes in O'Connor's writings, the author never explicitly argues why addressing the issue of shoes is important, so choice **A** is wrong. Choice **B** is the wrong answer because the passage focuses on works besides "A Late Encounter with the Enemy" and "Everything that Rises Must Converge." Also, the word "summarizes" in **B** suggests that the author's discussion of shoe imagery in "A Late Encounter" and "Everything that Rises" covers every use of shoe imagery in those stories, but the author never makes that implication in the passage. You can eliminate choice **C** because the author never suggests that the shoe imagery discussed in the passage is the most important shoe imagery in O'Connor's works, and you can eliminate choice **D** because the author never explicitly praises O'Connor.

2.   **C**

The passage opens with a statement that critics have tended to dismiss or ignore the issue of shoes in O'Connor's fiction. The author then disagrees with these critics by writing: "But in her work O'Connor draws the reader's attention to shoes so often that they should not be ignored." Since you know the author's reaction to these critics is negative, you can eliminate choice **A**, "surprised pleasure." You can also eliminate choices **B**, "mild annoyance," and **D**, "disbelief," since the author expresses neither annoyance nor astonishment. Choosing between **C**, "strong disagreement," and **E**, "unbridled anger," is a matter of distinguishing the degree to which the author reacts against the critics. Since the author's response is measured rather than passionate, **C** is the best answer to this question.

3. A

In order to answer this question, you simply need to go back to the second paragraph, where the author describes how Mrs. Turpin observes the shoes worn by people in the doctor's waiting room. Choice **A** is the right answer to this question. Be careful to read carefully because in the same paragraph, the author describes how characters on the bus in "Everything that Rises Must Converge" are described by their shoes. If you don't read carefully, you may be tempted to choose **D**.

4. B

Answering this question can be a little bit tricky, since you need to choose a difference that the author gives (in other words, directly states) rather than implies. You may think, for example, that you can infer choices **D** and **E** from the passage, but those answers are wrong because they are never explicitly stated in the passage. The only difference the author gives between Enoch and Sally is choice **B**. The author states this difference at the beginning of the fourth paragraph: "Other of her characters have a harder time discarding their identities than Enoch does." Then the author gives Sally an example of one of those characters.

5. D

Before you try to answer this question, you should go back to the passage and quickly glance over the second and third paragraphs. Because the paragraphs are related to each other, you should immediately eliminate choice **E**. You can also rule out choice **A**, because the third paragraph does not refute anything stated in the second, and choice **B**, because the third paragraph does not make a generalization (instead, it focuses on a specific example). Be wary of answer choices that use extreme phrases like "extend to their logical limits." While the third paragraph arguably does extend an argument made in the second paragraph, the argument made in the third paragraph does not reach a "logical limit." Choice **D** is the best answer to this question. The third paragraph develops the argument made in the second paragraph by adding another example to support the argument that O'Connor draws a connection between a person's shoes and his identity.

6. B

In lines 26–31, the author describes Sally's disappointment when she notices she is still wearing her Girl Scout shoes. The author writes: "Despite Sally's efforts to remake her appearance for the evening, her unsophisticated, clumsy shoes betray her true self." These lines suggest that Sally tries to make herself look elegant in the evening dress but that she fails because her shoes reveal how unsophisticated she really is. Choice **B** is the best answer to this question. You may be tempted to pick choice **E** because "ugly" and "bookish" are words attached to the girl in "Revelation" who also wears Girl Scout shoes, but because the question does not refer you to the second paragraph, **E** is the wrong answer to this question.

7. E

To answer this easy specific-information question, you should go back to the fifth paragraph, where the author discusses the peacock metaphor. The author writes: "The first notable use of the peacock metaphor occurred in the fourteenth century in *Piers Plowman*. In this poem, the peacock represents vanity." Reading the last sentence, you should see that choice **E** is the correct answer to this question.

8. C

This is a straightforward specific information question. If you don't remember what story Sally is in, you should go back to the fourth paragraph where she is mentioned for the first

the
new SAT
Critical
Reading
Workbook

123

time. The second sentence of that paragraph is: "In 'A Late Encounter with the Enemy,' Sally Poker Sash remembers attending the premiere of *Gone with the Wind* in Atlanta with her grandfather." Choice **C** is the correct answer.

9.   **D**

"Analogous to" means "similar to." If you don't know this definition, though, you can figure out the meaning of "analogous" from the context in which it's used. At the end of the fifth paragraph, the author writes that "the peacock's feet are analogous to Sally's shoes." The author then says that Sally lets vanity get the better of her, just as vanity got the better of the peacock when it realized that it had ugly feet. From these lines, you should be able to see that the peacock's feet and Sally's shoes are similar. Since you're looking for a word that suggests similarity, you can eliminate **A**, **B**, and **C**, all of which suggest difference. Choice **D** is a better answer than choice **E** because "the same as" is too strong a statement to describe the comparison made between the peacock's feet and Sally's shoes.

10.   **E**

The passage focuses on one aspect of Sally's relationship with her grandfather: how she uses him to show off. The author states: "By having him participate in the graduation ceremony, she hopes to show everyone that she has descended from an important family and that she is someone far above average." The correct answer to this question is **E**. Although Sally is clearly proud of her grandfather (otherwise she wouldn't want to show him off), choice **D** is wrong because she does not take good care of him. In fact, her callous treatment of her grandfather at her graduation results in his death: "The stress and the heat of the day prove too much for the old man, and when he is pushed on stage in his wheel chair, Sally Poker Sash sees that he has died in order to serve her vanity."

the
new SAT
Critical
Reading
Workbook

124

PRACTICE SET 12: LONG READING PASSAGE— ART

The following passage is an account of Pablo Picasso's art from 1906 to 1909.

Pablo Picasso soaked in all the experimental energy of the Parisian art scene and, inspired by other artists—especially Cézanne, and also the "primitive" art of Africa and the Pacific—Picasso began to create for himself a radically new style. In the summer of 1906, vacationing in a Catalan village, Picasso began carving wooden sculptures. In

5 these works, Picasso was driven to a simplification of form by both the technical properties of the wood he worked with and by the compelling memory of the prehistoric Spanish sculpture he had seen in the Louvre. His experience in wood-carving led to changes in his painting; his portrait of Gertrude Stein—in which he so radically simplified her face that it became the image of a chiseled mask—marks a crucial shift

10 in his painting. He stopped painting what he saw and started painting what he thought.

At the beginning of 1907, Picasso began a painting, "Les Demoiselles d'Avignon" ("The Young Women of Avignon"), which would become arguably the most important of the century. The painting began as a narrative brothel scene, with five prostitutes and

15 two men. But the painting metamorphosed as he worked on it; Picasso painted over the clients, leaving the five women to gaze out at the viewer, their faces terrifyingly bold and solicitous. The features of the three women to the left were inspired by the prehistoric sculpture that had interested Picasso the previous summer; those of the two to the right were based on the masks that he saw in the African and Oceanic collections

20 in a museum in Paris. Picasso was deeply impressed by what he saw in these collections, and they were to be one of his primary influences for the next several years.

Art historians once classified this phase of Picasso's work as his "Negro Period." French imperialism in Africa and the Pacific was at its high point, and gunboats and trading steamers brought back ritual carvings and masks as curiosities. While the

25 African carvings, which Picasso owned, had a kind of dignified aloofness, he, like other Europeans of his time, viewed Africa as the symbol of savagery. Unlike most Europeans, however, Picasso saw this savagery as a source of vitality and renewal that he wanted to incorporate in his painting. His interpretation of African art, in these mask-like faces, was based on this idea of African savagery; his brush-strokes are

30 hacking, impetuous, and violent.

"Les Demoiselles" was so shockingly new that Gertrude Stein called it "a veritable cataclysm." She meant this, of course, as a compliment. Not only did this painting later become a turning point duly remarked upon in every history of modern art, but Picasso felt at the time that his whole understanding of painting was revised in the course of

35 this canvas' creation.

In 1907, Picasso met Georges Braque, another young painter deeply interested in Cézanne. Braque and Picasso worked together closely; Braque later said they were "roped together like mountaineers" as they explored a new approach to organizing pictorial space. While Picasso had cleared the ground with "Les Demoiselles," Cubism

40 was a joint construction, to the extent that sometimes Picasso and Braque could not tell their work apart. Afterwards, describing Braque's role in Cubism's later evolution,

Picasso called him "just a wife," simultaneously dismissing both his colleague and women. But Braque's integral role in Cubism's initial invention cannot be disputed.

45 During the summer of 1908 Braque went to L'Estaque, in southern France, where his idol Cézanne had painted before him. The way in which Cubism attempted to see all angles at once, to paint an analysis of a form instead of its appearance, is illustrated by comparison of Braque's painting "Houses at L'Estaque" with a photograph of the view that Braque was painting. In the painting, scale and perspective are gone; forms are simplified into blocks. There is no distinction between foreground and background; the

50 shapes of the painting seem to be stacked on top of each other.

The influence of Braque and Cézanne is clear in Picasso's paintings from the summer of 1909, which he spent in Horta de Ebro. Braque and Picasso had extended Cézanne's method landscape painting to the point where a view became an almost monochromatic field of faceted form. This method led to paintings that were almost

55 indecipherable combinations of fragmented facets in grays and browns. Kahnweiler was later to name this stage of Picasso and Braque's work Analytical Cubism, because it was based on an analytical description of objects. Describing this period, Kahnweiler wrote, "The great step has been made. Picasso has exploded homogenous form." Indeed, Cubism was an explosion; not only did Cubist paintings resemble the shrapnel of their

60 ostensible subjects, but the intent was a kind of joyous destruction of the tradition of Western painting and the result was a revolution in art history.

1. According to the passage, the prehistoric Spanish sculpture Picasso saw at the Louvre inspired him to

(A) paint "Les Demoiselles d'Avignon"
(B) channel the savagery of African art into his painting
(C) explode homogeneous form
(D) explore Cubism with Georges Braque
(E) simplify the forms in his wooden sculptures

2. The word "metamorphosed" in line 15 most nearly means

(A) stalled
(B) grew worse
(C) developed
(D) became larger
(E) transformed

3. The "Negro Period" referred to in the third paragraph most likely derived its name from

(A) the period of French rule in Africa and the Pacific
(B) the collections which influenced Picasso at a museum in Paris
(C) the inspiration Picasso took from African and Pacific art
(D) the dress of the women depicted in "Les Demoiselles d'Avignon"
(E) Gertrude Stein's reaction to Picasso's new style of painting

4. The author most likely includes the sentence "She meant this, of course, as a compliment" in line 32 because the author wants to

(A) second Stein's praise of Picasso
(B) refute allegations that Stein's comment was mean-spirited
(C) chastise Stein for using abstruse language
(D) eliminate any ambiguity about Stein's comment
(E) praise Stein for her astute observations

the
new SAT
Critical
Reading
Workbook

126

5. The main purpose of the fifth paragraph is to

    (A) emphasize the role that Braque played in the evolution of Cubism
    (B) reveal Picasso as a selfish attention-seeker
    (C) credit Braque with the creation of Cubism
    (D) suggest that some paintings now attributed to Picasso were actually created by
        Braque
    (E) disparage Braque's role in the development of Cubism

6. The author refers to a comparison between Braque's painting and the photograph in lines 45–
    50 in order to

    (A) help the reader identify the content of the painting
    (B) emphasize the way the painting distorts conventional ways of seeing
    (C) demonstrate another link between Picasso and Braque
    (D) show how the painting epitomizes the endeavors of Cubism
    (E) underscore the differences between Braque's style of painting and Cézanne's

7. The author would most likely agree that Picasso's remark that Braque was "just a wife" (line
    42) is

    (A) an accurate assessment of the relationship
    (B) an attempt to steal fame from Braque
    (C) unfair and sexist
    (D) ironic
    (E) integral to understanding Picasso and Braque's relationship

8. According to the passage, how did Picasso's artistic style change during his "Negro Period"?

    (A) He moved away from painting representations of reality to painting
        representations of his ideas and thoughts.
    (B) He started working with wood sculpture instead of paint.
    (C) He depicted more complex forms in his art, gradually moving away from the
        simplification that had marked his earlier works.
    (D) He stopped producing European art and worked exclusively to create African and
        Pacific art.
    (E) He began to copy the Cubist style pioneered by Braque and Cézanne.

9. The main purpose of this passage is to

    (A) provide a biographical sketch of Picasso's life
    (B) examine the influence of Picasso's friends on his work
    (C) describe two stages of Picasso's artistic career
    (D) explain the significance of "Les Demoiselles d'Avignon" to modern art
    (E) argue that Braque deserves more credit than he receives for developing Cubism

10. It can be inferred from the passage that the importance of "Les Demoiselles d'Avignon" to
    twentieth-century art is that

    (A) it merged the business of French imperialism with the creation of art
    (B) it represented an acceptance of African and Pacific art in European cultural
        spheres
    (C) it shocked the public by explicitly depicting prostitutes in a brothel
    (D) its success made Picasso a famous, well-regarded painter
    (E) it marked a major stylistic change in Picasso's art and in art in general

ANSWERS & EXPLANATIONS

1. **E**

The answer to this question is in the first paragraph, which states, "Picasso was driven to a
simplification of form by both the technical properties of the wood he worked with and by the

compelling memory of the prehistoric Spanish sculpture he had seen in the Louvre." Using this sentence, you can identify the correct answer: **E**.

2. **E**

If you don't know the definition of "metamorphosed," you can answer this question using contextual clues. The sentence says, "the painting metamorphosed as he worked on it; Picasso painted over the clients, leaving the five women to gave out at the viewer." Since the second part of the sentence describes a drastic change that Picasso made to the painting, you can infer that "metamorphosed" means "changed." Of the answers, choice **E**, "transformed," is closest in meaning to "changed."

3. **C**

The last sentence of the second paragraph says that the African and Oceanic collections Picasso saw at a museum "were to be one of his primary influences for the next several years." Directly following this sentence, the next paragraph begins: "Art historians once classified this phase of Picasso's work as his 'Negro Period.'" These sentences suggest that this period derived its name from the inspiration Picasso took from African and Pacific art, so **C** is the best answer. While you may be tempted to choose **B**, you should remember that it was not the art itself that gave this period its name, but Picasso's use of the art.

4. **D**

This question asks you to identify the function of the sentence "She meant this, of course, as a compliment." The word "this" refers to Stein's comment quoted in the first sentence of the fourth paragraph: "'Les Demoiselles' was so shockingly new that Gertrude Stein called it 'a veritable cataclysm.'" The word "cataclysm" means "a moment of violent upheaval, demolition, and change," and depending on the context, it can have negative connotations. Since some people could interpret Stein's comment as a criticism of Picasso's art rather than as praise, the author of the passage is trying to explain Stein's comment and to remove any sense of ambiguity or uncertainty that Stein's comment could raise. The correct answer is **D**.

5. **A**

This question asks you to identify the author's intended point in the fifth paragraph. The paragraph focuses on Braque and Picasso's Cubist endeavors. The author writes that "Braque and Picasso worked closely" and that "Cubism was a joint construction." The last sentence of the paragraph states that "Braque's integral role in Cubism's initial invention cannot be disputed." These sentences indicate that the author is arguing that Cubism was a joint effort by Braque and Picasso, despite Picasso's later claims that Braque was "just a wife." The correct answer is **A**; the author is trying to emphasize that importance of Braque's involvement in Cubism without trying to overstate Braque's role.

6. **B**

The purpose of the author's comparison is to contrast the views of the painter and the photographic lens. The photograph ostensibly shows a normal view of the houses, in contrast to the view depicted by the painting, in which all angles are seen at once, perspective and scale disappear, and no distinction is made between foreground and background. Choice **B**, which says that the comparison shows how the painting distorts conventional ways of seeing, is correct. Although the comparison points to the style of the painting, the comparison does not show that the style is specifically Cubist, so don't be tempted by choice **D**.

the
new SAT
Critical
Reading
Workbook

128

7.   **C**

Although the author makes no explicit criticism of the remark, she points out how the remark is doubly insulting to Braque and women: "Picasso called him 'just a wife,' simultaneously dismissing both his colleague and women." The author makes it clear that **A** cannot be true by emphasizing the role Braque played in the evolution of Cubism. **B** is never implied in the passage, nor is **D**. Choice **E** tries to trick you by using a word ("integral") from later in the paragraph, but the author of the never implies that Picasso's statement is important to understanding his relationship with Braque. The correct answer is **B** because Picasso's statement unfairly diminishes Braque's involvement in Cubism and makes a sexist assumption about being a wife.

8.   **A**

Answering this question is a little tricky because the answer is in the first paragraph but the phrase "Negro Period" isn't mentioned until the third paragraph. You learn in the third paragraph that the period described in the beginning of the passage (the first four paragraphs) is called the "Negro Period" by art historians. In the first paragraph, the author states that during this period, Picasso "stopped painting what he saw and started painting what he thought." This sentence sums up how Picasso's artistic style changed during this period. Using this sentence, you can pick **A** as the best answer to the question. You can also try eliminating the other answer choices. You can immediately rule out choice **B** because according to this passage, Picasso does not stop painting in order to work exclusively with wood sculpture. You can also eliminate choice **C** since the passage focuses on how Picasso's style increasingly focused on simplified forms, the opposite of complex forms. You know that **D** is wrong because Picasso was only inspired by African art; he did not stop producing European art in order to create African art. Finally, you can rule out choice **E** since Cubism belongs to the stylistic period that follows the "Negro Period."

9.   **C**

While this passage touches on a number of issues—including events in Picasso's life, the influence of his friends, and the importance of "Les Demoiselles d'Avignon"—the main object of the passage is to describe two stages—the periods of primitivism and Analytical Cubism—in Picasso's art.

10.   **E**

The passage suggests that the significance of this painting to twentieth-century art arises from its newness—particularly its newness of style and execution. Of the answer choices, **E** is the best answer to the question. The painting marked a new style and a new understanding of art not only for Picasso but also, through Picasso's influence, for art in general.

sat

vocabulary

WHILE VOCABULARY IS LESS IMPORTANT ON THE NEW SAT, that doesn't mean it's totally unimportant. Not at all. A great vocabulary will definitely still help you on the test, especially throughout the Critical Reading section. So, despite what the press might say, the era of the SAT word isn't really over. You'll never again have to figure out how *horrid* relates to *horticulture* (it doesn't), but a good vocabulary *will* help boost your score on the Critical Reading and Writing sections of the new SAT.

REMEMBERING SAT VOCAB

Anyone can study vocabulary by reading over a list of words and definitions. Simple. But not that helpful. It's another thing entirely to *remember* the words you study.

Mnemonics

Mnemonic* devices are tricks of the memorizing trade. A mnemonic could be an image, a rhyme, a formula—anything other than straight repetition of a word and its definition. So, let's say you want to memorize the word *mnemonic*. You could come up with an image of the word *mnemonic* branded into some guy's brain as he correctly answers a Sentence Completion. The image will stick in your head much more readily than any dry old definition. With mnemonics, you'll remember words permanently and with less effort.

When you use mnemonics, the more outlandish the image or rhyme you can make up, the better. The farther out the mnemonic, the more sticky it will be in your brain. If you're trying to memorize the word *sacrosanct*, which means "holy, or something that should not be criticized," go all out. Imagine that scene in the *Raiders of the Lost Ark* when the holy "Ark of the Covenant" gets opened, and then everyone's face melts off because they dared to touch this holy, *sacrosanct* object. Boom. You know this word. You're not about to forget someone's face melting off. From now on, whenever you encounter an especially tough SAT vocab word, generate a detailed phrase or image that burns the meaning of the word into your memory.

Below are five mnemonic examples that we came up with to help you remember the definitions of some tough SAT vocab words:

SAT Word	Definition	Mnemonic	Word in a Sentence
buttress	a support	Having a big *butt* gives you extra support, like a *buttress*.	Without a strong *buttress*, the building's front structure would collapse.
conundrum	a problem or puzzle	Having only *one-drum* is a *conundrum* for a rock drummer.	The explorers figured out how to deal with the *conundrum* of having only two days to hike 100 miles.

---

* Pronounced *ni-'mä-nik*

the
new SAT
Critical
Reading
Workbook

133

cursory	brief and to the point	People tend to *curse* when they want to get straight to the point.	His boss took a *cursory* look at the memo and came to a decision.
malevolent	wanting harm to be done to others	*Violent males* tend to be *malevolent*.	The villain confirmed his *malevolent* wishes by cheering when the tree fell and crushed his neighbor's foot.
boon	a gift or blessing	Pirates consider booty a *boon*.	The teacher's decision to make the test open-book was a *boon* to her students.

Where the Wild Vocabs Are

SAT vocab lurks in lists and in life. You will be tempted to ignore life and focus only on the lists. That's up to you, but we think that's a mistake. You'll learn and retain more vocabulary if you focus on both.

Vocab in Lists

Studying vocab from a list of words seems easy, but it's actually quite tough. That list of words lulls you to sleep, so you think you're remembering what you study, but you're actually not. (This is another reason mnemonics are so helpful: You can't fool yourself into thinking you came up with a mnemonic. You've either got one or you don't.) You really need to focus to seal the meaning of the word into your mind. Breezing over a list won't make that happen.

There is another pitfall in studying vocab from lists. Your mind memorizes in context. One thing clues you into another. This can trick you into thinking that you know a word even when you don't—you may know it only when it's in the order from your list, not when it's sitting there alone in an answer choice. So, when you study from a list, don't always go through it in the same order. Switch things around, go backward, skip every other word. Keep your head on its toes. Or use flashcards and frequently reshuffle the deck.

Vocab in Life

Remember the other day when you were watching a movie like *The Matrix* and one of the characters said a word you didn't recognize, but you shrugged it off so you could just enjoy the show? Those days are over. From now until the day you take the new SAT, if you hear a word you don't know, try to guess its meaning from context, then look it up to see if you were right and make a mnemonic.

This takes some effort. And if you don't want to put out the effort to make the world your personal vocab oyster, well, we're not going to come track you down. But we will tell you that paying attention to words you encounter on lists *and* in life will go a long way toward building the vocabulary you need to beat the new SAT.

DEALING WITH WORDS YOU DON'T KNOW

No list will ever cover all the vocab words that might appear on the SAT. There are just too many words. In fact, we can pretty much guarantee that somewhere on the new SAT, you'll come across a word you haven't studied or just can't remember. No problem. We'll show you what to do.

Word Roots: The Building Blocks of Words

Lots of test-prep companies advise students to study Greek and Latin roots of English words to help figure out the meaning of an SAT vocabulary word. Some students even take Latin in high school with the sole aim of using it to learn vocabulary roots for the SAT. English words are often made up of bits and pieces derived from Latin or Greek, which we call *word roots*. For example, let's say you come across the word *antebellum* on the SAT and don't know what it means. The word root *ante* means "before," and *bellum* means "war," so you might think that antebellum means "before the war." You're correct! Here's a list of the 28 most common word roots that'll help you puzzle out the meanings of unfamiliar SAT words.

Word Root	What It Means	SAT Vocab Words
ante	before	antebellum, antediluvian
anti	against	antithesis, antipathy, antiseptic
auto	self	autocratic
bene	good, well	benefactor, benevolent, benediction
chron	time	anachronism, asynchronous
circum	around	circumnavigate, circumference, circumlocution, circumvent, circumscribe
con, com	with, together	convene, confluence, concatenate, conjoin
contra, counter	against	contradict, counteract, contravene
cred	to believe	credo, credible, credence, credulity, incredulous
dict	to speak	verdict, malediction, dictate, dictum, indict
dis	not	disperse, dissuade, distemper, disarray, disjointed
equi	equal	equidistant, equilateral, equilibrium, equinox, equitable, equanimity
ex, e	out, away	emit, enervate, excise, extirpate, expunge, exonerate, exacerbate
flu, flux	flow	effluence, effluvium, fluctuate, confluence
hyper	above, over	hyperbolic
in, im	not	inviolate, innocuous, intractable, impregnable, impermeable, impervious
inter	between	intermittent, introvert, interdict, interrogate
mal	bad	malformation, maladjusted, dismal, malady, malcontent, malfeasance
multi	many	multitude, multivalent
neo	new	neologism, neophyte
omni	all	omnipotent, omnivorous, omniscient
per	through	persuade, impervious, persistent, persecute
sanct	holy	sanctify, sanctuary, sanction, sanctimonious, sacrosanct
scrib, script	to write	inscription, prescribe, proscribe, ascribe, conscript, scribble, scribe
spect	to look	circumspect, retrospect, prospect, spectacle, aspect
tract	to drag, to draw	protract, detract, intractable
trans	across	transduce, intransigent
vert	to turn	extrovert, introvert

THE TOP 250 MOST DIFFICULT SAT WORDS

THE TOP 250

Since vocab isn't as important on the new SAT as it was on the old SAT, it doesn't make sense to plow through 1,000-word-long lists. We're dedicated to getting you the most bang for your study time, so we searched through tons of old SAT tests and found 250 of the toughest and most frequently tested vocab words.

Of course, we know there'll be some of you out there who just can't get enough and who want the complete collection of 1,000 words. Well, we've got those for you also, free and online. Just go to **http://www.sparknotes.com** to download and memorize to your heart's content.

A

abjure *(v.)* to reject, renounce *(To prove his honesty, the president abjured the evil policies of his wicked predecessor.)*

abrogate *(v.)* to abolish, usually by authority *(The Bill of Rights assures that the government cannot abrogate our right to a free press.)*

acerbic *(adj.)* biting, bitter in tone or taste *(Jill became extremely acerbic and began to cruelly make fun of all her friends.)*

acrimony *(n.)* bitterness, discord *(Though they vowed that no girl would ever come between them, Biff and Trevor could not keep acrimony from overwhelming their friendship after they both fell in love with the lovely Teresa.)*

acumen *(n.)* keen insight *(Because of his mathematical acumen, Larry was able to figure out in minutes problems that took other students hours.)*

adumbrate *(v.)* to sketch out in a vague way *(The coach adumbrated a game plan, but none of the players knew precisely what to do.)*

alacrity *(n.)* eagerness, speed *(For some reason, Chuck loved to help his mother whenever he could, so when his mother asked him to set the table, he did so with alacrity.)*

anathema *(n.)* a cursed, detested person *(I never want to see that murderer. He is an anathema to me.)*

antipathy *(n.)* a strong dislike, repugnance *(I know you love me, but because you are a liar and a thief, I feel nothing but antipathy for you.)*

approbation *(n.)* praise *(The crowd welcomed the heroes with approbation.)*

arrogate *(v.)* to take without justification *(The king arrogated the right to order executions to himself exclusively.)*

ascetic *(adj.)* practicing restraint as a means of self-discipline, usually religious *(The priest lives an ascetic life devoid of television, savory foods, and other pleasures.)*

the
new SAT
**Critical
Reading
Workbook**

137

aspersion (*n.*) a curse, expression of ill-will (*The rival politicians repeatedly cast aspersions on each others' integrity.*)

assiduous (*adj.*) hard-working, diligent (*The construction workers erected the skyscraper during two years of assiduous labor.*)

B

blandish (*v.*) to coax by using flattery (*Rachel's assistant tried to blandish her into accepting the deal.*)

boon (*n.*) a gift or blessing (*The good weather has been a boon for many businesses located near the beach.*)

brusque (*adj.*) short, abrupt, dismissive (*The captain's brusque manner offended the passengers.*)

buffet 1. (*v.*) to strike with force (*The strong winds buffeted the ships, threatening to capsize them.*) 2. (*n.*) an arrangement of food set out on a table (*Rather than sitting around a table, the guests took food from our buffet and ate standing up.*)

burnish (*v.*) to polish, shine (*His mother asked him to burnish the silverware before setting the table.*)

buttress 1. (*v.*) to support, hold up (*The column buttresses the roof above the statue.*) 2. (*n.*) something that offers support (*The buttress supports the roof above the statues.*)

C

cacophony (*n.*) tremendous noise, disharmonious sound (*The elementary school orchestra created a cacophony at the recital.*)

cajole (*v.*) to urge, coax (*Fred's buddies cajoled him into attending the bachelor party.*)

calumny (*n.*) an attempt to spoil someone else's reputation by spreading lies (*The local official's calumny ended up ruining his opponent's prospect of winning the election.*)

capricious (*adj.*) subject to whim, fickle (*The young girl's capricious tendencies made it difficult for her to focus on achieving her goals.*)

clemency (*n.*) mercy (*After he forgot their anniversary, Martin could only beg Maria for clemency.*)

cogent (*adj.*) intellectually convincing (*Irene's arguments in favor of abstinence were so cogent that I could not resist them.*)

concomitant (*adj.*) accompanying in a subordinate fashion (*His dislike of hard work carried with it a concomitant lack of funds.*)

conflagration (*n.*) great fire (*The conflagration consumed the entire building.*)

contrite (*adj.*) penitent, eager to be forgiven (*Blake's contrite behavior made it impossible to stay angry at him.*)

conundrum (*n.*) puzzle, problem (*Interpreting Jane's behavior was a constant conundrum.*)

the
new SAT
Critical
Reading
Workbook

138

credulity (*n.*) readiness to believe (*His <u>credulity</u> made him an easy target for con men.*)

cupidity (*n.*) greed, strong desire (*His <u>cupidity</u> made him enter the abandoned gold mine despite the obvious dangers.*)

cursory (*adj.*) brief to the point of being superficial (*Late for the meeting, she cast a <u>cursory</u> glance at the agenda.*)

D

decry (*v.*) to criticize openly (*The kind video rental clerk <u>decried</u> the policy of charging customers late fees.*)

defile (*v.*) to make unclean, impure (*She <u>defiled</u> the calm of the religious building by playing her banjo.*)

deleterious (*adj.*) harmful (*She experienced the <u>deleterious</u> effects of running a marathon without stretching her muscles enough beforehand.*)

demure (*adj.*) quiet, modest, reserved (*Though everyone else at the party was dancing and going crazy, she remained <u>demure</u>.*)

deprecate (*v.*) to belittle, depreciate (*Always over-modest, he <u>deprecated</u> his contribution to the local charity.*)

deride (*v.*) to laugh at mockingly, scorn (*The bullies <u>derided</u> the foreign student's accent.*)

desecrate (*v.*) to violate the sacredness of a thing or place (*They feared that the construction of a golf course would <u>desecrate</u> the preserved wilderness.*)

desiccated (*adj.*) dried up, dehydrated (*The skin of the <u>desiccated</u> mummy looked like old paper.*)

diaphanous (*adj.*) light, airy, transparent (*Sunlight poured in through the <u>diaphanous</u> curtains, brightening the room.*)

diffident (*adj.*) shy, quiet, modest (*While eating dinner with the adults, the <u>diffident</u> youth did not speak for fear of seeming presumptuous.*)

discursive (*adj.*) rambling, lacking order (*The professor's <u>discursive</u> lectures seemed to be about every subject except the one initially described.*)

dissemble (*v.*) to conceal, fake (*Not wanting to appear heartlessly greedy, she <u>dissembled</u> and hid her intention to sell her ailing father's stamp collection.*)

dither (*v.*) to be indecisive (*Not wanting to offend either friend, he <u>dithered</u> about which of the two birthday parties he should attend.*)

E

ebullient (*adj.*) extremely lively, enthusiastic (*She became <u>ebullient</u> upon receiving an acceptance letter from her first-choice college.*)

effrontery (*n.*) impudence, nerve, insolence (*When I told my aunt that she was boring, my mother scolded me for my <u>effrontery</u>.*)

effulgent (*adj.*) radiant, splendorous (*The golden palace was <u>effulgent</u>.*)

egregious *(adj.)* extremely bad *(The student who threw sloppy joes across the cafeteria was punished for his egregious behavior.)*

enervate *(v.)* to weaken, exhaust *(Writing these sentences enervates me so much that I will have to take a nap after I finish.)*

ephemeral *(adj.)* short-lived, fleeting *(She promised she'd love me forever, but her "forever" was only ephemeral: she left me after one week.)*

eschew *(v.)* to shun, avoid *(George hates the color green so much that he eschews all green food.)*

evanescent *(adj.)* fleeting, momentary *(My joy at getting promoted was evanescent because I discovered that I would have to work much longer hours in a less friendly office.)*

evince *(v.)* to show, reveal *(Christopher's hand-wringing and nail-biting evince how nervous he is about the upcoming English test.)*

exculpate *(v.)* to free from guilt or blame, exonerate *(My discovery of the ring behind the dresser exculpated me from the charge of having stolen it.)*

execrable *(adj.)* loathsome, detestable *(Her pudding is so execrable that it makes me sick.)*

exigent *(adj.)* urgent, critical *(The patient has an exigent need for medication, or else he will lose his sight.)*

expiate *(v.)* to make amends for, atone *(To expiate my selfishness, I gave all my profits to charity.)*

expunge *(v.)* to obliterate, eradicate *(Fearful of an IRS investigation, Paul tried to expunge all incriminating evidence from his tax files.)*

extant *(adj.)* existing, not destroyed or lost *(My mother's extant love letters to my father are in the attic trunk.)*

extol *(v.)* to praise, revere *(Violet extolled the virtues of a vegetarian diet to her meat-loving brother.)*

F

fallacious *(adj.)* incorrect, misleading *(Emily offered me cigarettes on the fallacious assumption that I smoked.)*

fastidious *(adj.)* meticulous, demanding, having high and often unattainable standards *(Mark is so fastidious that he is never able to finish a project because it always seems imperfect to him.)*

fatuous *(adj.)* silly, foolish *(He considers himself a serious poet, but in truth, he only writes fatuous limericks.)*

fecund *(adj.)* fruitful, fertile *(The fecund tree bore enough apples to last us through the entire season.)*

feral *(adj.)* wild, savage *(That beast looks so feral that I would fear being alone with it.)*

fetid *(adj.)* having a foul odor *(I can tell from the fetid smell in your refrigerator that your milk has spoiled.)*

the
new SAT
Critical
Reading
Workbook

140

florid *(adj.)* flowery, ornate *(The writer's <u>florid</u> prose belongs on a sentimental Hallmark card.)*

fractious *(adj.)* troublesome or irritable *(Although the child insisted he wasn't tired, his <u>fractious</u> behavior—especially his decision to crush his cheese and crackers all over the floor—convinced everyone present that it was time to put him to bed.)*

G

garrulous *(adj.)* talkative, wordy *(Some talk-show hosts are so <u>garrulous</u> that their guests can't get a word in edgewise.)*

grandiloquence *(n.)* lofty, pompous language *(The student thought her <u>grandiloquence</u> would make her sound smart, but neither the class nor the teacher bought it.)*

gregarious *(adj.)* drawn to the company of others, sociable *(Well, if you're not <u>gregarious</u>, I don't know why you would want to go to a singles party!)*

H

hackneyed *(adj.)* unoriginal, trite *(A girl can only hear "I love you" so many times before it begins to sound <u>hackneyed</u> and meaningless.)*

hapless *(adj.)* unlucky *(My poor, <u>hapless</u> family never seems to pick a sunny week to go on vacation.)*

harangue 1. *(n.)* a ranting speech *(Everyone had heard the teacher's <u>harangue</u> about gum chewing in class before.)* 2. *(v.)* to give such a speech *(But this time the teacher <u>harangued</u> the class about the importance of brushing your teeth after chewing gum.)*

hegemony *(n.)* domination over others *(Britain's <u>hegemony</u> over its colonies was threatened once nationalist sentiment began to spread around the world.)*

I

iconoclast *(n.)* one who attacks common beliefs or institutions *(Jane goes to one protest after another, but she seems to be an <u>iconoclast</u> rather than an activist with a progressive agenda.)*

ignominious *(adj.)* humiliating, disgracing *(It was really <u>ignominious</u> to be kicked out of the dorm for having an illegal gas stove in my room.)*

impassive *(adj.)* stoic, not susceptible to suffering *(Stop being so <u>impassive</u>; it's healthy to cry every now and then.)*

imperious *(adj.)* commanding, domineering *(The <u>imperious</u> nature of your manner led me to dislike you at once.)*

impertinent *(adj.)* rude, insolent *(Most of your comments are so <u>impertinent</u> that I don't wish to dignify them with an answer.)*

impervious *(adj.)* impenetrable, incapable of being affected *(Because of their thick layer of fur, many seals are almost <u>impervious</u> to the cold.)*

impetuous *(adj.)* rash; hastily done *(Hilda's hasty slaying of the king was an <u>impetuous</u>, thoughtless action.)*

impinge 1. *(v.)* to impact, affect, make an impression *(The hail impinged the roof, leaving large dents.)* 2. *(v.)* to encroach, infringe *(I apologize for impinging upon you like this, but I really need to use your bathroom. Now.)*

implacable *(adj.)* incapable of being appeased or mitigated *(Watch out: Once you shun Grandma's cooking, she is totally implacable.)*

impudent *(adj.)* casually rude, insolent, impertinent *(The impudent young man looked the princess up and down and told her she was hot even though she hadn't asked him.)*

inchoate *(adj.)* unformed or formless, in a beginning stage *(The country's government is still inchoate and, because it has no great tradition, quite unstable.)*

incontrovertible *(adj.)* indisputable *(Only stubborn Tina would attempt to disprove the incontrovertible laws of physics.)*

indefatigable *(adj.)* incapable of defeat, failure, decay *(Even after traveling 62 miles, the indefatigable runner kept on moving.)*

ineffable *(adj.)* unspeakable, incapable of being expressed through words *(It is said that the experience of playing with a dolphin is ineffable and can only be understood through direct encounter.)*

inexorable *(adj.)* incapable of being persuaded or placated *(Although I begged for hours, Mom was inexorable and refused to let me stay out all night after the prom.)*

ingenuous *(adj.)* not devious; innocent and candid *(He must have writers, but his speeches seem so ingenuous it's hard to believe he's not speaking from his own heart.)*

inimical *(adj.)* hostile *(I don't see how I could ever work for a company that was so cold and inimical to me during my interviews.)*

iniquity *(n.)* wickedness or sin *("Your iniquity," said the priest to the practical jokester, "will be forgiven.")*

insidious *(adj.)* appealing but imperceptibly harmful, seductive *(Lisa's insidious chocolate cake tastes so good but makes you feel so sick later on!)*

intransigent *(adj.)* refusing to compromise, often on an extreme opinion *(The intransigent child said he would have 12 scoops of ice cream or he would bang his head against the wall until his mother fainted from fear.)*

inure *(v.)* to cause someone or something to become accustomed to a situation *(Twenty years in the salt mines inured the man to the discomforts of dirt and grime.)*

invective *(n.)* an angry verbal attack *(My mother's irrational invective against the way I dress only made me decide to dye my hair green.)*

inveterate *(adj.)* stubbornly established by habit *(I'm the first to admit that I'm an inveterate coffee drinker—I drink four cups a day.)*

J

jubilant *(adj.)* extremely joyful, happy *(The crowd was jubilant when the firefighter carried the woman from the flaming building.)*

juxtaposition *(n.)* the act of placing two things next to each other for implicit comparison *(The interior designer admired my juxtaposition of the yellow couch and green table.)*

L

laconic *(adj.)* terse in speech or writing *(The author's laconic style has won him many followers who dislike wordiness.)*

languid *(adj.)* sluggish from fatigue or weakness *(In the summer months, the great heat makes people languid and lazy.)*

largess *(n.)* the generous giving of lavish gifts *(My boss demonstrated great largess by giving me a new car.)*

latent *(adj.)* hidden, but capable of being exposed *(Sigmund's dream represented his latent paranoid obsession with other people's shoes.)*

legerdemain *(n.)* deception, slight-of-hand *(Smuggling the French plants through customs by claiming that they were fake was a remarkable bit of legerdemain.)*

licentious *(adj.)* displaying a lack of moral or legal restraints *(Marilee has always been fascinated by the licentious private lives of politicians.)*

limpid *(adj.)* clear, transparent *(Mr. Johnson's limpid writing style greatly pleased readers who disliked complicated novels.)*

M

maelstrom *(n.)* a destructive whirlpool which rapidly sucks in objects *(Little did the explorers know that as they turned the next bend of the calm river a vicious maelstrom would catch their boat.)*

magnanimous *(adj.)* noble, generous *(Although I had already broken most of her dishes, Jacqueline was magnanimous enough to continue letting me use them.)*

malediction *(n.)* a curse *(When I was arrested for speeding, I screamed maledictions against the policeman and the entire police department.)*

malevolent *(adj.)* wanting harm to befall others *(The malevolent old man sat in the park all day, tripping unsuspecting passersby with his cane.)*

manifold *(adj.)* diverse, varied *(The popularity of Dante's* Inferno *is partly due to the fact that the work allows for manifold interpretations.)*

maudlin *(adj.)* weakly sentimental *(Although many people enjoy romantic comedies, I usually find them maudlin and shallow.)*

mawkish *(adj.)* characterized by sick sentimentality *(Although some nineteenth-century critics viewed Dickens's writing as mawkish, contemporary readers have found great emotional depth in his works.)*

mendacious *(adj.)* having a lying, false character *(The mendacious content of the tabloid magazines is at least entertaining.)*

mercurial (*adj.*) characterized by rapid change or temperamentality (*Though he was widely respected for his mathematical proofs, the mercurial genius was impossible to live with.*)

modicum (*n.*) a small amount of something (*Refusing to display even a modicum of sensitivity, Henrietta announced her boss's affair in front of the entire office.*)

morass (*n.*) a wet swampy bog; figuratively, something that traps and confuses (*When Theresa lost her job, she could not get out of her financial morass.*)

multifarious (*adj.*) having great diversity or variety (*This Swiss Army knife has multifarious functions and capabilities. Among other things, it can act as a knife, a saw, a toothpick, and a slingshot.*)

munificence (*n.*) generosity in giving (*The royal family's munificence made everyone else in their country rich.*)

myriad (*adj.*) consisting of a very great number (*It was difficult to decide what to do Friday night because the city presented us with myriad possibilities for fun.*)

N

nadir (*n.*) the lowest point of something (*My day was boring, but the nadir came when I accidentally spilled a bowl of spaghetti on my head.*)

nascent (*adj.*) in the process of being born or coming into existence (*Unfortunately, my brilliant paper was only in its nascent form on the morning that it was due.*)

nefarious (*adj.*) heinously villainous (*Although Dr. Meanman's nefarious plot to melt the polar icecaps was terrifying, it was so impractical that nobody really worried about it.*)

neophyte (*n.*) someone who is young or inexperienced (*As a neophyte in the literary world, Malik had trouble finding a publisher for his first novel.*)

O

obdurate (*adj.*) unyielding to persuasion or moral influences (*The obdurate old man refused to take pity on the kittens.*)

obfuscate (*v.*) to render incomprehensible (*The detective did not want to answer the newspaperman's questions, so he obfuscated the truth.*)

oblique (*adj.*) diverging from a straight line or course, not straightforward (*Martin's oblique language confused those who listened to him.*)

obsequious (*adj.*) excessively compliant or submissive (*Mark acted like Janet's servant, obeying her every request in an obsequious manner.*)

obstreperous (*adj.*) noisy, unruly (*Billy's obstreperous behavior prompted the librarian to ask him to leave the reading room.*)

obtuse (*adj.*) lacking quickness of sensibility or intellect (*Political opponents warned that the prime minister's obtuse approach to foreign policy would embroil the nation in mindless war.*)

odious (*adj.*) instilling hatred or intense displeasure (*Mark was assigned the odious task of cleaning the cat's litter box.*)

officious *(adj.)* offering one's services when they are neither wanted nor needed *(Brenda resented Allan's <u>officious</u> behavior when he selected colors that might best improve her artwork.)*

opulent *(adj.)* characterized by rich abundance verging on ostentation *(The <u>opulent</u> furnishings of the dictator's private compound contrasted harshly with the meager accommodations of her subjects.)*

ostensible *(adj.)* appearing as such, seemingly *(Jack's <u>ostensible</u> reason for driving was that airfare was too expensive, but in reality, he was afraid of flying.)*

P

palliate *(v.)* to reduce the severity of *(The doctor trusted that the new medication would <u>palliate</u> her patient's discomfort.)*

pallid *(adj.)* lacking color *(Dr. Van Helsing feared that Lucy's <u>pallid</u> complexion was due to an unexplained loss of blood.)*

panacea *(n.)* a remedy for all ills or difficulties *(Doctors wish there was a single <u>panacea</u> for every disease, but sadly there is not.)*

paragon *(n.)* a model of excellence or perfection *(The mythical Helen of Troy was considered a <u>paragon</u> of female beauty.)*

pariah *(n.)* an outcast *(Following the discovery of his plagiarism, Professor Hurley was made a <u>pariah</u> in all academic circles.)*

parsimony *(n.)* frugality, stinginess *(Many relatives believed that my aunt's wealth resulted from her <u>parsimony</u>.)*

pathos *(n.)* an emotion of sympathy *(Martha filled with <u>pathos</u> upon discovering the scrawny, shivering kitten at her door.)*

paucity *(adj.)* small in quantity *(Gilbert lamented the <u>paucity</u> of twentieth-century literature courses available at the college.)*

pejorative *(adj.)* derogatory, uncomplimentary *(The evening's headline news covered an international scandal caused by a <u>pejorative</u> statement the famous senator had made in reference to a foreign leader.)*

pellucid *(adj.)* easily intelligible, clear *(Wishing his book to be <u>pellucid</u> to the common man, Albert Camus avoided using complicated grammar when composing* The Stranger.*)*

penurious *(adj.)* miserly, stingy *(Stella complained that her husband's <u>penurious</u> ways made it impossible to live the lifestyle she felt she deserved.)*

perfidious *(adj.)* disloyal, unfaithful *(After the official was caught selling government secrets to enemy agents, he was executed for his <u>perfidious</u> ways.)*

perfunctory *(adj.)* showing little interest or enthusiasm *(The radio broadcaster announced the news of the massacre in a surprisingly <u>perfunctory</u> manner.)*

pernicious *(adj.)* extremely destructive or harmful *(The new government feared that the Communist sympathizers would have a <u>pernicious</u> influence on the nation's stability.)*

perspicacity (*adj.*) shrewdness, perceptiveness (*The detective was too humble to acknowledge that his* perspicacity *was the reason for his professional success.*)

pertinacious (*adj.*) stubbornly persistent (*Harry's parents were frustrated with his* pertinacious *insistence that a monster lived in his closet. Then they opened the closet door and were eaten.*)

petulance (*n.*) rudeness, irritability (*The nanny resigned after she could no longer tolerate the child's* petulance.)

pithy (*adj.*) concisely meaningful (*My father's long-winded explanation was a stark contrast to his usually* pithy *statements.*)

platitude (*n.*) an uninspired remark, cliché (*After reading over her paper, Helene concluded that what she thought were profound insights were actually just* platitudes.)

plethora (*n.*) an abundance, excess (*The wedding banquet included a* plethora *of oysters piled almost three feet high.*)

polemic (*n.*) an aggressive argument against a specific opinion (*My brother launched into a* polemic *against my arguments that capitalism was an unjust economic system.*)

portent (*n.*) an omen (*When a black cat crossed my sister's path while she was walking to school, she took it as a* portent *that she would do badly on her spelling test.*)

precocious (*adj.*) advanced, developing ahead of time (*Derek was so academically* precocious *that by the time he was 10 years old, he was already in the ninth grade.*)

prescient (*adj.*) to have foreknowledge of events (*Questioning the fortune cookie's prediction, Ray went in search of the old hermit who was rumored to be* prescient.)

primeval (*adj.*) original, ancient (*The first primates to walk on two legs, called* Australopithecus, *were the* primeval *descendants of modern man.*)

probity (*n.*) virtue, integrity (*Because he was never viewed as a man of great* probity, *no one was surprised by Mr. Samson's immoral behavior.*)

proclivity (*n.*) a strong inclination toward something (*In a sick twist of fate, Harold's childhood* proclivity *for torturing small animals grew into a desire to become a surgeon.*)

promulgate (*v.*) to proclaim, make known (*The film professor* promulgated *that both in terms of sex appeal and political intrigue, Sean Connery's James Bond was superior to Roger Moore's.*)

propensity (*n.*) an inclination, preference (*Dermit has a* propensity *for dangerous activities such as bungee jumping.*)

propitious (*adj.*) favorable (*The dark storm clouds visible on the horizon suggested that the weather would not be* propitious *for sailing.*)

prosaic (*adj.*) plain, lacking liveliness (*Heather's* prosaic *recital of the poem bored the audience.*)

the
new SAT
Critical
Reading
Workbook

146

proscribe (*v.*) to condemn, outlaw (*The town council voted to proscribe the sale of alcohol on weekends.*)

protean (*adj.*) able to change shape; displaying great variety (*Among Nigel's protean talents was his ability to touch the tip of his nose with his tongue.*)

prurient (*adj.*) eliciting or possessing an extraordinary interest in sex (*David's mother was shocked by the discovery of prurient reading material hidden beneath her son's mattress.*)

puerile (*adj.*) juvenile, immature (*The judge demanded order after the lawyer's puerile attempt to object by stomping his feet on the courtroom floor.*)

pugnacious (*adj.*) quarrelsome, combative (*Aaron's pugnacious nature led him to start several barroom brawls each month.*)

pulchritude (*n.*) physical beauty (*Several of Shakespeare's sonnets explore the pulchritude of a lovely young man.*)

punctilious (*adj.*) eager to follow rules or conventions (*Punctilious Bobby, hall monitor extraordinaire, insisted that his peers follow the rules.*)

Q

quagmire (*n.*) a difficult situation (*We'd all like to avoid the kind of military quagmire characterized by the Vietnam War.*)

querulous (*adj.*) whiny, complaining (*If deprived of his pacifier, young Brendan becomes querulous.*)

quixotic (*adj.*) idealistic, impractical (*Edward entertained a quixotic desire to fall in love at first sight in a laundromat.*)

R

rancor (*n.*) deep, bitter resentment (*When Eileen challenged me to a fight, I could see the rancor in her eyes.*)

rebuke (*v.*) to scold, criticize (*When the cops showed up at Sarah's party, they rebuked her for disturbing the peace.*)

recalcitrant (*adj.*) defiant, unapologetic (*Even when scolded, the recalcitrant young girl simply stomped her foot and refused to finish her lima beans.*)

rectitude (*n.*) uprightness, extreme morality (*The priest's rectitude gave him the moral authority to counsel his parishioners.*)

replete (*adj.*) full, abundant (*The unedited version was replete with naughty words.*)

reprobate (*adj.*) evil, unprincipled (*The reprobate criminal sat sneering in the cell.*)

reprove (*v.*) to scold, rebuke (*Lara reproved her son for sticking each and every one of his fingers into the strawberry pie.*)

repudiate (*v.*) to reject, refuse to accept (*Kwame made a strong case for an extension of his curfew, but his mother repudiated it with a few biting words.*)

rescind (*v.*) to take back, repeal (*The company rescinded its offer of employment after discovering that Jane's resume was full of lies.*)

restive *(adj.)* resistant, stubborn, impatient *(The restive audience pelted the band with mud and yelled nasty comments.)*

ribald *(adj.)* coarsely, crudely humorous *(While some giggled at the ribald joke involving a parson's daughter, most sighed and rolled their eyes.)*

rife *(adj.)* abundant *(Surprisingly, the famous novelist's writing was rife with spelling errors.)*

ruse *(n.)* a trick *(Oliver concocted an elaborate ruse for sneaking out of the house to meet his girlfriend while simultaneously giving his mother the impression that he was asleep in bed.)*

S

sacrosanct *(adj.)* holy, something that should not be criticized *(In the United States, the Constitution is often thought of as a sacrosanct document.)*

sagacity *(n.)* shrewdness, soundness of perspective *(With remarkable sagacity, the wise old man predicted and thwarted his children's plan to ship him off to a nursing home.)*

salient *(adj.)* significant, conspicuous *(One of the salient differences between Alison and Nancy is that Alison is a foot taller.)*

sanctimonious *(adj.)* giving a hypocritical appearance of piety *(The sanctimonious Bertrand delivered stern lectures on the Ten Commandments to anyone who would listen, but thought nothing of stealing cars to make some cash on the side.)*

sanguine *(adj.)* optimistic, cheery *(Polly reacted to any bad news with a sanguine smile and the chirpy cry, "When life hands you lemons, make lemonade!")*

scurrilous *(adj.)* vulgar, coarse *(When Bruno heard the scurrilous accusation being made about him, he could not believe it because he always tried to be nice to everyone.)*

serendipity *(n.)* luck, finding good things without looking for them *(In an amazing bit of serendipity, penniless Paula found a $20 bill in the subway station.)*

servile *(adj.)* subservient *(The servile porter crept around the hotel lobby, bowing and quaking before the guests.)*

solicitous *(adj.)* concerned, attentive *(Jim, laid up in bed with a nasty virus, enjoyed the solicitous attentions of his mother, who brought him soup and extra blankets.)*

solipsistic *(adj.)* believing that oneself is all that exists *(Colette's solipsistic attitude completely ignored the plight of the homeless people on the street.)*

somnolent *(adj.)* sleepy, drowsy *(The somnolent student kept falling asleep and waking up with a jerk.)*

spurious *(adj.)* false but designed to seem plausible *(Using a spurious argument, John convinced the others that he had won the board game on a technicality.)*

staid *(adj.)* sedate, serious, self-restrained *(The staid butler never changed his expression no matter what happened.)*

the
new SAT
Critical
Reading
Workbook

148

stolid *(adj.)* expressing little sensibility, unemotional *(Charles's stolid reaction to his wife's funeral differed from the passion he showed at the time of her death.)*

stupefy *(v.)* to astonish, make insensible *(Veronica's audacity and ungratefulness stupefied her best friend, Heather.)*

surfeit *(n.)* an overabundant supply or indulgence *(After partaking of the surfeit of tacos and tamales at the All-You-Can-Eat Taco Tamale Lunch Special, Beth felt rather sick.)*

surmise *(v.)* to infer with little evidence *(After speaking to only one of the students, the teacher was able to surmise what had caused the fight.)*

surreptitious *(adj.)* stealthy *(The surreptitious CIA agents were able to get in and out of the house without anyone noticing.)*

sycophant *(n.)* one who flatters for self-gain *(Some see the people in the cabinet as the president's closest advisors, but others see them as sycophants.)*

T

tacit *(adj.)* expressed without words *(I interpreted my parents' refusal to talk as a tacit acceptance of my request.)*

taciturn *(adj.)* not inclined to talk *(Though Jane never seems to stop talking, her brother is quite taciturn.)*

tantamount *(adj.)* equivalent in value or significance *(When it comes to sports, fearing your opponent is tantamount to losing.)*

temerity *(n.)* audacity, recklessness *(Tom and Huck entered the scary cave armed with nothing but their own temerity.)*

tenuous *(adj.)* having little substance or strength *(Your argument is very tenuous, since it relies so much on speculation and hearsay.)*

timorous *(adj.)* timid, fearful *(When dealing with the unknown, timorous Tallulah almost always broke into tears.)*

torpid *(adj.)* lethargic, dormant, lacking motion *(The torpid whale floated, wallowing in the water for hours.)*

tractable *(adj.)* easily controlled *(The horse was so tractable, Myra didn't even need a bridle.)*

transient *(adj.)* passing through briefly; passing into and out of existence *(Because virtually everyone in Palm Beach is a tourist, the population of the town is quite transient.)*

transmute *(v.)* to change or alter in form *(Ancient alchemists believed that it was possible to transmute lead into gold.)*

trenchant *(adj.)* effective, articulate, clear-cut *(The directions that accompanied my new cell phone were trenchant and easy to follow.)*

truculent *(adj.)* ready to fight, cruel *(This club doesn't really attract the dangerous types, so why was that bouncer being so truculent?)*

turgid *(adj.)* swollen, excessively embellished in style or language *(The haughty writer did not realize how we all really felt about his turgid prose.)*

turpitude (*n.*) depravity, moral corruption (*Sir Marcus's chivalry often contrasted with the <u>turpitude</u> he exhibited with the ladies at the tavern.*)

U

ubiquitous (*adj.*) existing everywhere, widespread (*It seems that everyone in the United States has a television. The technology is <u>ubiquitous</u> here.*)

umbrage (*n.*) resentment, offense (*He called me a lily-livered coward, and I took <u>umbrage</u> at the insult.*)

unctuous (*adj.*) smooth or greasy in texture, appearance, manner (*The <u>unctuous</u> receptionist seemed untrustworthy, as if she was only being helpful because she thought we might give her a big tip.*)

undulate (*v.*) to move in waves (*As the storm began to brew, the placid ocean began to <u>undulate</u> to an increasing degree.*)

upbraid (*v.*) to criticize or scold severely (*The last thing Lindsay wanted was for Lisa to <u>upbraid</u> her again about missing the rent payment.*)

usurp (*v.*) to seize by force, take possession of without right (*The rogue army general tried to <u>usurp</u> control of the government, but he failed because most of the army backed the legally elected president.*)

V

vacillate (*v.*) to fluctuate, hesitate (*I prefer a definite answer, but my boss kept <u>vacillating</u> between the distinct options available to us.*)

vacuous (*adj.*) lack of content or ideas, stupid (*Beyoncé realized that the lyrics she had just penned were completely <u>vacuous</u> and tried to add more substance.*)

vapid (*adj.*) lacking liveliness, dull (*The professor's comments about the poem were surprisingly <u>vapid</u> and dull.*)

variegated (*adj.*) diversified, distinctly marked (*Each wire in the engineering exam was <u>variegated</u> by color so that the students could figure out which one was which.*)

venerate (*v.*) to regard with respect or to honor (*The tribute to John Lennon sought to <u>venerate</u> his music, his words, and his legend.*)

veracity (*n.*) truthfulness, accuracy (*With several agencies regulating the reports, it was difficult for Latifah to argue against its <u>veracity</u>.*)

verdant (*adj.*) green in tint or color (*The <u>verdant</u> leaves on the trees made the world look emerald.*)

vex (*v.*) to confuse or annoy (*My little brother <u>vexes</u> me by poking me in the ribs for hours on end.*)

vicarious (*adj.*) experiencing through another (*All of my lame friends learned to be social through <u>vicarious</u> involvement in my amazing experiences.*)

vicissitude (*n.*) event that occurs by chance (*The <u>vicissitudes</u> of daily life prevent me from predicting what might happen from one day to the next.*)

vilify (v.) to lower in importance, defame (*After the Watergate scandal, almost any story written about President Nixon sought to <u>vilify</u> him and criticize his behavior.*)

viscous (adj.) not free flowing, syrupy (*The <u>viscous</u> syrup took three minutes to pour out of the bottle.*)

vitriolic (adj.) having a caustic quality (*When angry, the woman would spew <u>vitriolic</u> insults.*)

vituperate (v.) to berate (*Jack ran away as soon as his father found out, knowing he would be <u>vituperated</u> for his unseemly behavior.*)

W

wanton (adj.) undisciplined, lewd, lustful (*Vicky's <u>wanton</u> demeanor often made the frat guys next door very excited.*)

winsome (adj.) charming, pleasing (*After such a long, frustrating day, I was grateful for Chris's <u>winsome</u> attitude and childish naivete.*)

wistful (adj.) full of yearning; musingly sad (*Since her pet rabbit died, Edda missed it terribly and was <u>wistful</u> all day long.*)

wizened (adj.) dry, shrunken, wrinkled (*Agatha's grandmother, Stephanie, had the most <u>wizened</u> countenance, full of leathery wrinkles.*)

Z

zenith (n.) the highest point, culminating point (*I was too nice to tell Nelly that she had reached the absolute <u>zenith</u> of her career with that one hit of hers.*)

zephyr (n.) a gentle breeze (*If not for the <u>zephyrs</u> that were blowing and cooling us, our room would've been unbearably hot.*)